# HIGHBURY COUNTY
## REVISITED

*The Church Missionary Society's children's home in circa 1855 (Photo from
the Victoria County History of Middlesex, Vol. VIII)
Below: Highbury School in the mid 1960s shortly before demolition
(Photo: London Metropolitan Archives)*

# *Highbury County Revisited*

by Brian Boyle

edited with additional material
by David Perman

Rockingham Press

First published 2005
by The Rockingham Press
11 Musley Lane,
Ware, Herts SG12 7EN

**A catalogue record of this book is available
from the British Library**

**ISBN 1-904851-010**

Printed in Great Britain by
Biddles Limited
Kings Lynn

# *Dedication*

*To the Memory of those Old Highburians*
*who are no longer with us.*

# *Foreword*

*There is a tide in the affairs of men,*
*which taken at the flood, leads on to fortune ...*
*Julius Caesar* – William Shakespeare

It began as a friendly challenge thrown down over a pint in the pub by my old schoolmate one evening when our conversation turned, as it has so often done over the years, to reminiscence about former school-pals. He suggested that trying to find "a few of them" would give me something to do in my early retirement. After forty-five years, it was a bit of a tall order, I said.

Still, a dare is just as much a dare today as it was all those years ago, and I couldn't lose face now! Amongst the papers, which I had inherited from my parents, was the programme for the School Dramatic Society's 1953 production of *Morning Departure* and cuttings from the local papers of the time. Armed with this list of names, I contacted Gill Whitley in Anglesey, who carries out the computer research for the "Missing & Found" feature in the *Daily Mail*. She advised me that she could not undertake to reunite me with as many people as appeared on the cast list, but would gladly provide lists of matching names from around the country, for me to follow up. I was very soon in touch with Tony Sandell and Pat Hartigan, who put me in touch with a few more, and so the ripple effect set in. Pretty soon we were in contact with over fifty Old Boys. When the "Friends Reunited" web-site was launched, contacts increased dramatically. It appeared that we had quite unknowingly latched on to a wave of nostalgia amongst people of our generation, which we were pleasantly surprised to see manifested in the support for the Reunion functions.

Old Alumnus David Perman suggested that in view of the plethora of school magazines, old photos and anecdotal letters we have amassed, we should compile and edit it all to provide a lasting record of our schooldays. This book is our legacy. Five years ago, a small group of us agreed to resurrect the Old Highburians for a Reunion, where we hoped to revive the *esprit de corps* of the Highbury County we remember. This, then is our attempt to honour our old watchword: *Ne Absiste* – "Never abstain" (from effort, that is to say! )

Many people have helped in the preparation of this book, by lending us photographs, by sending us their recollections, by offering advice and generally giving us support and encouragement. We thank them all. Particular thanks is given to some of them, including copyright holders of photographs, on page 160.

Brian Boyle

# Contents

## Chapter One
# *How it was : a Highbury Timeline*

The name "Highbury" first appears in two documents of circa 1340 and 1444. Prior to this, the area had been called "Newington Barrow', and it is unclear whether the place took its name from the de Barowe family who owned the manor, or vice versa. The manor house was on the hilltop at the top of Highbury Grove, in Leigh Road, roughly where the block of flats called Eton House has stood since World War II. The name "Highbury" distinguished it from the lower lying manor houses of either Canonbury or Barnsbury and Holloway. In 1271 Lady Alicia de Barowe gave the manor to the Order of the Knights of St. John of Jerusalem who established a moated manor house and farm at what is now called "Highbury Barn".

**1381**, June: the Prior's Highbury manor house was destroyed during the Peasants' Revolt and for the next 500 years the derelict site was known as "Jack Straw's Castle" after the legendary leader of the rebels – with far more justification than the other "Jack Straw's Castle" in Hampstead.

**1542**, following the Dissolution of Monasteries and Priories, Henry VIII granted the Manor of Highbury to Sir Henry Knevett; in 1629 it passed to Sir Allen Apaley; in 1723 it was alienated to James Colebrook, who bequeathed it to Sir George Colebrook (1729-1809), a City banker and member of the East India Company.

**1781,** the manor was sold to John Dawes, a wealthy stockbroker who erected Highbury House at a cost of £10,000, and resided there until his death in 1788. The manor house was demolished in 1938 and the Eton House flats were built on the site. During John Dawes' lifetime, between 1774-79 Highbury Place had been built, with Highbury Crescent added later on the opposite side of Highbury Fields. Highbury Grove appears in Rate Books as early as 1796. Thus it was that Highbury became established as a residential area of considerable prestige.

**1848**: Christ Church, situated in Highbury Grove and opposite Highbury Hill, was consecrated by the Bishop of London. Despite the nearness of the Highbury Barn pleasure gardens (which succeeded Vauxhall as the summer entertainment venue for middle class Londoners) Highbury was now firmly in the embrace of Evangelical Christianity emanating from St. Mary's in Upper Street, Islington. Thus it is no surprise that the Church Missionary Society also moved to Highbury.

**1850**: Henry Ryton, an ex-tailor from Finsbury Circus and owner of brickfields at Ware in Hertfordshire, began developing the Highbury New Park Estate. The houses had spacious plots and the name came from attempts to establish a large public park in the area, similar to Victoria Park in Hackney. Most residents had their own businesses: the 1861 Census shows that all but four per cent of the households had at least one servant and the wealthier ones up to six. The poet John Betjeman lived in Highbury New Park as a boy and wrote about it in a poem entitled "St. Saviour's, Aberdeen Park, Highbury, London, N":

> *These were the streets my parents knew when they loved and won —*
> *The brougham that crunched the gravel, the laurel-girt paths that wind,*
> *Geranium-beds for the lawn, Venetian blinds for the sun,*
> *A separate tradesman's entrance, straw in the mews behind,*
> *Just in the four-mile radius where the hackney carriages run,*
> *Solid Italianate houses for the solid commercial mind.*

**1853**: the Church Missionary Society built an imposing four-storey children's home near the junction of Highbury Grove and Highbury New Park. The CMS acquired the land from the estate of Richard Laycock who died in 1834.

**1887**: Queen Victoria's Golden Jubilee, only surpassed in pomp by the Diamond Jubilee in 1897.

**1891**: the children's home became a residential school for persistent truants. School attendance had been made compulsory by the 1870 Education Act but many older children stayed away, often with their parents' knowledge. The Highbury Truant School, under Superintendent George Thomas Peall, was like an American "boot camp" with a harsh and despotic discipline.

**1900** brought a new century, with Britain embroiled in war with the Boers in South Africa, and in 1901 Queen Victoria died and Edward VII acceded to the throne. In 1902 the war ended and peace returned. In that year the Northern Polytechnic established a secondary school elsewhere in Islington, and so began the history of the school later known as Highbury County.

**1909**: the school became the Highbury Industrial School for child delinquents. Probably during this era the art and woodwork rooms were erected in a block at the rear of the main building, together with an indoor swimming pool and purpose built Gymnasium on the Highbury New Park side of the main building.

**1922**: the London County Council took over the school which the Northern Polytechnic had established and transferred it to the former Children's Home building in Highbury Grove, where it was renamed as "Highbury County School". The historic link with the Northern Polytechnic is preserved to this day in the colours of the Old Highburians necktie: on a field of navy blue, a diagonal red stripe, bordered by two narrow stripes in gold. These were the

*Above: physical jerks in the south playground at the Highbury Truant School (Reproduced by kind permission from "Islington Past" by John Richardson, published in 2000 by Historical Publications, 32 Ellington Street, London, N7 8PL) Below: the school in a leafy Edwardian setting in 1908 (Photo from "Images of England : Islington 2nd Selection" by Gavin Smith, published by Tempus Publishing Ltd.)*

original sporting colours of the Northern Polytechnic. When their sports teams were transferred to Highbury, their sporting prowess seems so to have impressed the College that they were happy for the boys of Highbury County to continue to appear in their colours. The crest with the purple, black and white colours, and the Latin motto "Ne Absiste" (from Virgil's Aeneid, meaning "Don't Give Up") which are more familiar to most of us, were introduced by Mr. R.J. Marsh, MA, Headmaster from 1928 to 1953.

> When the London County Council opened the new Highbury County School in 1922 Mr. William Spragg was appointed as the first Headmaster. Harry H. Bloom (92), who started at Highbury in 1923, recalled Mr. Spragg as "a very good man and an excellent teacher."The late Alfred Arthur Wright who died in 2004 and Len Clarke (now 88) who both started their education at Highbury in 1925, described him somewhat differently, however as "being over kindly, and with not much discipline. Incidentally the School moved from Holloway Road to what had been a Truant School in Aberdeen Park, converted into a Grammar School." Alfred recalled being punished for some misdemeanour by Mr. Spragg, who awarded Alf a punishment of SIX LINES. When Alf duly handed in this impost, Mr. Spragg patted him on the shoulder, and complimented him on his handwriting! Perhaps this accounts for his relatively short tenure in the post.

**1924**, April: one hundred thousand people were present when King George V inaugurated the British Empire Exhibition at Wembley. In July of that same year the King reviewed the Atlantic and Reserve Fleets, comprising some 196 warships anchored off Spithead, with pendants and flags fluttering as a salute of 21 guns was fired. During 1925 and 1926 there were industrial troubles in the coalmines, and in May 1926 workers in many industries went on strike to support the miners, resulting in what became known as the General Strike.

**1925**, September: Mr. T.R. Kemplen joined the staff as teacher of Chemistry and Woodwork. At the end of the First World War he held the rank of Lieutenant in the Royal Engineers (Signals), a rank which he would resume in the Home Guard in the Second World War. Before long he was to demonstrate a much wider range of talents. An Appreciation published in *The Highburian Magazine*, January 1956, following his retirement the previous year records:

> Between 1925 and 1954 more than fifteen hundred boys must have left Highbury School. Some will remember Mr. Kemplen for his Woodwork, some for his Latin, and some others for his Chemistry and Physics; so varied were his interests and qualifications. The effective sets, which he constructed for school plays – notably for R.U.R. (in 1931) – are still recorded in old photographs. Members of Canonbury House past and present will not forget his willing leadership. Cricketers will remember his lusty hitting in Staff vs.

School matches. His older colleagues remembered his sincerity and humility, and a quality perhaps less definable, his unexpectedness. From him a witty remark, a queer (sic) anecdote, an obscure bit of erudition, or even a song could, by its rarity and aptness, set his friends rocking.

**1926**: Mr. Phillip Howells came to Highbury from Hereford as an assistant master teaching French. Two years later by a very wise choice, he was made Second Master. Very young for such a responsible appointment, he brought to the position his genius for organisation, fair play and management of the staff and boys. On his retirement in 1954, *The Highburian Magazine* published an appreciation of his contribution to the School. "From 1926 to 1954 Highbury was an outpost of a Swansea dominated empire. How gladly we bore our yoke, and how sadly we will surrender it."

**1927**, April (St. George's Day): Arsenal Football Club played their first Cup Final against Cardiff City at Wembley. King George V, Lord Derby and Winston Churchill were among the 90,000 spectators, of whom 10,000 were Welshmen. Phillip Howells' loyalties must have been somewhat divided, for although Arsenal were the favourites, and did most of the attacking, the only goal of the match was scored by Ferguson for Cardiff.

**1928**, September: Mr. R.J. Marsh, MA came from Sheffield to Highbury as Headmaster. Before going to Sheffield he had been on the staff of Worksop College, then one of our Public Schools. He set about reorganising the school. Alf Wright recalled that "Mr. Marsh introduced a reign of terror" after his arrival, "with queues of boys outside his study, waiting to be caned." The boys soon accepted his more disciplined regime, and he was soon affectionately known, if behind his back, as "The Bog," or simply, "Boggy."

Alfred also recalled Mr. 'Viv' Gage, the Sports master, Mr. Chapman, Mr. Garrett who taught him History, and Mr. Howells – "who had a Welsh accent, by the way." Also there at that time were a Mr. Davis, and a Miss Bradley, who taught music.

Alfred Wright continued, "Both Mr. Garrett and Mr. Howells expected me to get distinctions in History and French. But I got only 60% in both subjects. I remember the Science masters, 'Sam' Golding and Mr. Kemplen, who had a motor car in 1928! In those days you hardly ever saw a car in Highbury!"

Alf also recalled: "Mr. Garrett, when taking the Detention Book, asked, 'Who was the boy who gave me the book?' 'Beer, Sir,' I replied, Mr. Garrett said, 'I wish it was!'"

"We played cricket and football at Higham's Park. I cannot be sure now whether it was 'Sam' Golding or Mr. Howells who sent us from Hackney Downs station to Enfield! What a mess!" Higham's Park, of course was nowhere near Enfield!

The earliest artefacts to come into our possession are the programme for the Annual Prize Distribution, which was held at the Northern Polytechnic on Thursday 20 December 1928, together with *The Highburian Magazine* edition for Vol. II No 7 of March 1929.

### *The 1928 Prize Distribution & School Play*

The evening event started at 7.00 p.m. with an organ recital by D. Knights, which lasted until 7.30, followed by Part Songs, "Viking's Song" and "Pilgrim's Song," performed by the School. Next O.F. Flint gave a Recitation of "Keats in Rabbit Land." A Pianoforte solo of Liszt's "Liebestraum" by D. Knights followed this.

Then followed two more Part Songs, "Sweet and Low," and "Fall on me," performed by the choir. A solo, "Awake" was then performed by K.J. Fowler, a recitation from "Richard III" was then given by one of the pupils, named Hayes. This then led to the Finale, "The Soldiers' Chorus," by Gounod, which was sung by the whole school.

Alderman Sidney C. Harper, JP, the Mayor of Islington, then distributed the Prizes; ten Form Prizes, thirty-five Subject Prizes, the Special Essay Prize, and a Public Service Prize, presented by the Old Boys. Mr. R.L. Roberts, the Chairman of the Governors, then rose and proposed that Mr. Marsh should read his report of the year's work.

The Headmaster commenced by saying that naturally he was "more than a little diffident at having to present to parents a report on the year's work, when he had been in the school for only three months". He mentioned that a new playing field had been acquired at Higham's Park, "although as yet the school had not had the opportunity of enjoying this acquisition."

The evening concluded with a performance of George Bernard Shaw's *The Devil's Disciple* in three acts, produced by Dr. Smith and Mr. Chapman. Mr. Kemplen was the Stage Manager. Nine members of the cast signed our copy of the Programme. The production received the following review in *The Highburian Magazine*:

"… the most ambitious attempt made yet by the School's Dramatic Society, and the culmination of one of the most co-operative efforts in the history of the School ... But for Mr. Kemplen the whole project would have had to be abandoned, as there was no money for the hiring of scenery and properties, which the play demanded. In the end we were left uncertain for which to be more grateful – the many hours of arduous work done by him, or his cleverness in devising expedients for overcoming seemingly insuperable obstacles." The review concluded: "One or two have queried

*The Highburian Magazine for March 1929 (left) and July 1939.*

whether a two hour entertainment was worth this protracted effort and expense. From every point of view the answer is in the affirmative."

In its editorial, *The Highburian Magazine* reported:

"The extremely severe weather experienced since our last issue, and the consequently high numbers of absences, among both staff and pupils, have led this year to a break in one of the traditions of the School. It has been decided that the Annual Examination shall be postponed until the Summer Term. This does not however, apply to the Matriculation forms, who will as usual receive their tests at the end of the present session; a wise provision in view of the approaching Matriculation Examinations. It must be confessed that this breach with tradition did not unduly disturb the majority of the Middle and Lower schools; may they adequately justify the respite so unexpectedly granted them."

**1929** Mr. Donald Collins Leech came to Highbury as Senior English Master. An Appreciation of his contribution to the School on his retirement in 1955 in *The Highburian Magazine* of July 1956 records that: "His vigorous and enterprising spirit would never allow him to rest content with running the English department and Finsbury House efficiently. His organising ability was at once shown in the first of a long succession of full-scale plays that he produced every year with the somewhat meagre talent available in a boys' school. His ability in casting was extraordinary and the confidence, which he shared with Burbage that a boy could be taught to play a girl's role, was often fully justified. There is no doubt that the theatre was his first love; indeed it has been said that he dramatised all his lessons. Some of his older colleagues could testify that even in the Staff room, his play at the Bridge table was highly dramatic – if over acted at times."

**1931**: the Revd. E.G. Taylor – school chaplain and divinity teacher – arranged the first School Camp at Seaton in Devon, a tradition which apart from the War years, was to continue until the 1960s. In March 1932 *The Highburian Magazine* reported: "The numbers of the School continue to increase, and it is expected that the Summer Term will see a fifth Second Form. We hope to repeat last year's experiment with a Summer Camp at Seaton in Devon."

**1933**, 31 January: the National Socialist Party was elected to power in Germany, with Adolf Hitler as Chancellor. In Britain Sir Oswald Mosley's British Union of Fascists held rallies in London, and his "Blackshirts" marched provocatively through the streets in London's East End. In July 1933 Alfred Wright gained his Matriculation and left Highbury County to start his first job in an insurance company. We shall learn more of Alfred's life and times in "the Cloak & Dagger War," later in this book.

**1934**, March: *The Highburian Magazine* carried a report which seems to indicate that the School was increasing its numbers and catchment area. "The four houses which have existed since our opening as Highbury County in 1922, have now been converted into six: Clissold, Finsbury, Isledon and Tuffnell have now given place to Barnsbury, Canonbury, City, Finsbury, Highbury and Stoke Newington." The houses were later reduced to four again.

**1938**, 12 July: The Islington Gazette of that date carried a report about the school.

### Highbury County School
### LCC's Rebuilding Proposal

A report to be submitted by the Education Committee at today's Meeting of the London County Council observes:

The programme 1935-38 included a proposal for a new school to replace Highbury County School, and on the 27th July 1937 the Council approved a capital estimate of £21,500 for the extension of the site of the school to permit of the erection of the new premises. We have now approved the preliminary plans of the new buildings.

The new school, which will accommodate 450-530 boys, will be sited mainly on the additional land, and with the exception of a portion at the south-west corner, can be erected while the existing building remains in occupation. All the existing buildings will be demolished, with the exception of one of the properties to be acquired, which is a two-storey house, recently erected, and which we propose to retain for the use of the schoolkeeper. ...

The total estimated cost, including incidental expenses, layout of the site, and the supply of furniture and equipment, is £57,815. The approximate incidence of expenditure will be £1,000 in 1938-39, £24,000 in 1939-40, £24,000 in 1940-41 and £8,815 in 1941-42. ... The Committee recommended that the estimate of £57,815, in respect of the layout of the site and the supply of furniture and equipment, be approved.

**1938** was a year of crisis. On 12 March German troops entered Austria and two days later Hitler announced its annexation (*Anschluss*) to the Reich. In September, with the possibility of war over German claims on the Sudetenland (the German-speaking parts of Czechoslovakia), Prime Minister Neville Chamberlain returned from his meeting with Hitler in Munich, flourishing a piece of paper to the newsreel cameras which he told the nation promised "Peace in our time." German troops occupied the Sudetenland two days later. In November came *Krystallnacht* (the Night of Broken Glass) when Nazi mobs in Germany smashed windows and set fire to Jewish businesses and synagogues. Many Jewish families made arrangements to leave German occupied countries – among those now considering leaving Vienna were the Burstin, Glasberg and Jagendorf families. Tragically some would leave it too late.

On 1 November 1938 the following report appeared in the *Islington Gazette*. Mr. Marsh's theme is as pertinent to life sixty-seven years later, as it was then.

### Headmaster's Plea to Parents
### "Help Us to Make Democratic Citizens"

#### Mr. Marsh's Remarks at Highbury County Prize-giving

A plea to parents to help the schools in making democratic citizens of the future was made by Mr. R.J. Marsh, MA., Headmaster of Highbury County School, when speaking at the annual Speech Day, held at the Northern Polytechnic on Thursday.

Giving his report, Mr. Marsh said: "I want to make an appeal to all thinking parents. Some people are very rightly worrying a great deal about the future of democracy and telling us schoolmasters that democracy depends entirely upon the Schools. I do not think so. Schools can be the strength of dictators, for we see them devoted to producing that docile, herd-like spirit essential to the dictator. But a people fit for freedom must have not only the right kind of school, but also the right kind of home.

"For example, we are expected to teach citizenship to our boys; – I must say that any boy who has a normal home, and who is a cheerful and helpful member of the family, has learnt the most elementary lesson of citizenship. For home is his real point of contact with life, and there lies his best preparation for the wider contacts of later life.

## "Personal religion needed"

"Above all I feel that the element in democracy that especially needs the home is personal religion. That is the only thing that can fight this materialistic docility of a people ripe for dictatorship.

"To us in this country, the individual is still real and what matters is whether that individual minds the things of God or of Man. If of Man, then he is condemned in slavery to self as his supreme aim in life. If of God, then he will look beyond mere material satisfaction to the good of all. So I beg of you to help keep alive in your boys every impulse towards a spiritual outlook, a sense of principle and a capacity for judgement. There you will find the School doing its best to help you, and you will be helping the School. The price of liberty is not eternal talk, or even eternal vigilance; it is eternal service."

**1939**: As the year opened, Kenneth Lockwood Bass and Eric Voller had just completed their first term at Highbury. It was Eric who lent us *The Highburian Magazine* for July, 1939, the last to appear until after the war. The editors were H. Gavourin and D.L. Mayes. The magazine reported a better cricket season than last year's, progress on cataloguing the School Library (which had just received all the "Just William" books), a debate in the previous issue between "E.G.T." and "H.G." (Messrs. Taylor and Golding) over the compatibility of science and religion, and a contribution entitled STOP PRESS by Prefect A.R. Hammond, in which he said "there will not be a new school after all" and "a boy in the wash house was seen to (i) wash his hands; (ii) wash his face; (iii) wash his knees; (iv) rinse out the basin; (v) replace the towel."

On 3 September 1939, Britain declared war on Germany. In the same month, Highbury County School moved to Kimbolton, then in Huntingdonshire. In 1939 it would have been quite a small place, dominated by its castle, then part of the estates of the Montagu family, Dukes of Manchester. It was in an earlier version of the castle that Katharine of Aragon, Henry VIII's first Queen, was incarcerated from 1534 until her death in 1536. The present castle was and is

# HIGHBURY COUNTY SCHOOL

## News From Somerset

The boys of Highbury County School, happily settled at Midsomer Norton, Somerset, send their greetings to all their kind friends in Islington and district.

They have been at Midsomer Norton since December last, their first adventure into the wilds of Huntingdonshire landing them in an area singularly lacking in secondary accommodation. After a patient wait of three months to be moved to almost every town of any size in the area, the magic carpet appeared in the shape of an L.M.S. train and whisked them away to Somerset.

EXAM. RESULTS

They soon settled down to full time regular work, and it is perhaps the best testimony to boys and staff that only six months' work could produce results in keeping with those of past years. Eighty-six per cent. of the entries gained School Certificate, 100 per cent. Higher Certificate, while R. Lacey was awarded a State scholarship for the rare feat of gaining four distinctions.

With the neighbouring schools the various cricket and football teams have more than held their own; Oliver Hills, in particular, distinguishing himself by a fine century against a strong Midsomer Norton men's side. The boys have much appreciated having a Sports Field within easy reach for games.

Unfortunately, in July last, the passage of aeroplanes on their way to attack South Wales caused many parents to take fright, and they argued that London was safer! Many thus condemned their boys to the London "Blitz" instead of leaving them to go quietly on with their work. It is perhaps relevant to remind any such parents who may be reading this that since the School started its Autumn Term on September 1st no time whatever has been lost from school hours.

WORK ON FARMS

In the "holidays" much valuable and vital work has been done on farms especially in August and September. One big farmer was good enough to say that if he could have ten boys like those he had at Easter, he wanted no others from other schools.

Instead of the usual school camp at Seaton, Mr. E. G. Taylor organised three camps on Exmoor, which were so successful that the Somerset War Agricultural Committee asked especially for the camps to be allowed to continue an extra three weeks. This Christmas some of the boys are going lumbering for Lord Hylton in Ammerdown Park.

The usual Carol Concert was held last week and much enjoyed. One particular out-of-school activity has been the "Friday Club," organised by Mr. Leech, in which the boys meet every Friday for games and discussions.

HEALTH EXCELLENT

The health of the boys is on the whole excellent; the great majority of foster-parents have been most kind.

To all Old Boys the School sends its best wishes, and hopes that all on active service will write to the Headmaster (R. J. March, M.A.), Highbury County School, at Midsomer Norton, Somerset, and inform him of their doings. One Old Boy, Sergeant H. Davis has been awarded the D.F.C. A very prominent sportsman in "Bill" Meredith died in hospital recently from wounds received in France.



*"News from Somerset" – the Islington Gazette of 27 December 1940 reported that the school had settled in well at Midsomer Norton, Somerset, "after their first adventure into the wilds of Huntingdonshire" landed them in an area singularly lacking in secondary accomodation. Unfortunately (the report went on) in July 1940 "the passage of aeroplanes on their way to attack South Wales caused many parents to take fright and they argued that London was safer! The report was intended to reassure other London parents that Somerset was safe. The school had done well against local teams at football and cricket; and Mr. E.G. Taylor had organised three successful camps on Exmoor for agricultural work.*

a splendid structure, designed by among others Vanbrugh, Hawksmoor and Robert Adam, but in 1939 it was requisitioned by the Royal Army Medical Corps – Highbury was to use the village school at the far end of the village. Today this is the Preparatory School for the Public School, which has occupied the Castle since the Duke emigrated to Kenya in 1950.

Kenneth Lockwood Bass attended Highbury from 1938 to 1945. He was evacuated with the school to Kimbolton. There was insufficient room at Kimbolton to billet all the boys and hold sufficient classes. Thus it fell to the French master, Phillip Howells to arrange their accommodation and to co-ordinate their lessons, spread around the nearby towns of St. Neots and Huntingdon. These towns are about ten miles apart, on what was then the Great North Road, while Kimbolton lies to the West, some seven miles distant from either along winding country roads. Legend has it that Mr. Howells covered this 25-mile round trip every day on a bicycle, ensuring that every boy was comfortable and had a class to attend. Mr. Howells must have experienced great relief in December 1939, when the school was moved to Midsomer Norton in Somerset, where more suitable quarters were made available.

**1940**, July: Kenneth Bass and his younger brother, Ivor returned home to London. This had been the "phoney war" period, when the much-dreaded mass bombing of London and other cities, as shown in cinema newsreels about Poland and France, had not materialised. Many evacuees were emboldened to return to their families in London at this time, just in time for the real *Blitz*.

**1942**: an Emergency Grammar School reopened at the William Ellis School at Parliament Hill, to cope with the number of boys who had become weary of evacuation and had returned home to London. Phillip Howells returned to London to act as Headmaster of that school. Those among the staff who were privileged to return with him were later to look back on this time as "the Golden Age." So many evacuees were returning to London by this time, that many London schools were reopened. Although Highbury County School had sustained some bomb damage, it was repaired and reopened in September 1943. Kenneth Bass then returned to the School, where he sat the Higher Schools Certificate Examination in July 1945, just before he was 18.

**1951**: the Government decided to restore public morale after years of wartime shortages, rationing and austerity. To mark the centenary of the Great Exhibition of 1851, as well as to give Britain's manufacturing industries a boost, the Festival of Britain was held on the South Bank of the Thames in Southwark. Streets of bomb-damaged houses and warehouses were cleared between Waterloo Bridge and County Hall, to be replaced by new edifices such as the Royal Festival Hall, the Dome of Discovery, the "Skylon" and exhibition buildings, where Britain's latest technology was to be displayed. The progress of this building work could be seen from Hemingford Road in Barnsbury.

**1952**, February: King George VI died of cancer shortly after bidding farewell to his daughter Princess Elizabeth at London Airport, when she and Prince Philip flew off to Kenya on holiday. The following day she flew back to London with her husband and set foot on English soil again as Queen Elizabeth II. George Cobby remembered that Mr. Marsh rented a televison set so that boys in every form should see at least 20 minutes of King George's funeral. The Coronation of the young Queen was held on 2 June 1953, and parties of children from schools everywhere were allocated places in hastily constructed stands along the route of the procession through the streets of London. With the party from Highbury was sixth-former Philip Blumenthal, who reported for the July Edition of *The Highburian Magazine*:

A Coronation is indeed a rare event and to all of us in the School party it was an entirely novel one. We set out then to make the most of the chance which had been given us to see the procession.

Leaving the school very promptly at six o'clock in the morning, we travelled by Tube train to Waterloo, and arrived on the North bank at about half-past seven. We were greeted by a great procession of Marines with a raucous naval band at their head, marching along the Embankment. Under the guidance of Mr. Chapman and Mr. Rosenthal, we were then taken to our allotted place, and prepared for the long wait.

For a June morning the weather was particularly foul; dark clouds covered the sky and it was only by pulling up our collars and wearing scarves that we were able to keep warm.

The LCC, exercising their usual foresight and efficiency promptly dealt with the situation by issuing a cold drink and following that with an ice lollipop. Their generosity was not riotously acclaimed.

But nobody allowed either the weather or the LCC to spoil such a day, and when the Lord Mayor passed in a beautiful golden coach we knew that the spectacle was about to start. From then until eleven o'clock we saw the glorious procession pass along to the Abbey. Streams of cars conveying foreign ambassadors and representatives, state coaches with colonial rulers and the chiefs of the armed forces.

Many colonial regiments, mounted and on foot were represented, and provided the brilliant colours which were so memorable. Finally column after column of the Guards marched past, heralding the approach of the Queen's carriage.

As soon as it appeared, coming majestically down the Victoria Embankment on our left, a deafening roar arose. Taking several minutes to pass us, the coach was cheered and acclaimed enthusiastically by all of us lining the route. From within the Queen graciously acknowledged the cheers;

she looked so radiantly beautiful, very happy and not a little overwhelmed by the deafening reception. We had seen what we had come to see.

## Blooming Good Days at Highbury

The following is a transcription in full of a letter received from Mr. Harry Bloom, (92) former Sales Director of Gross Cash Registers. I was approached by an Old William Ellis-ian, who remembers playing football with Ken Bass and some others of us, and who discovered only recently that his long-time friend, Harry is an Old Highburian. He arranged for me to phone Harry at his home in West Hampstead. Harry has wonderful recall, is a great conversational wit, as I found when I met him over the phone in February '04. As he is undoubtedly our oldest fellow alumnus, I respectfully invite you to read his story for yourselves:

"I became a pupil at Highbury County at the age of ten – eighty years ago. (Actually in 1923, he told me) My late Dad was in the Royal Flying Corps in the 1914-18 War, and had to pay for my education, which cost him £4 a term and was a strain at this time. We could not afford the luxury of football boots or white trousers for cricket. The Gym master was a Sergeant Mills in the War; a very tough gentleman with a heart of gold. As I'm still here eighty years later, his discipline must have worked.

"The Headmaster, Mr. Spragg, was a perfectionist in English lessons and made most of the pupils lovers of Shakespeare, and was the epitome of a gentleman. Our form master, Mr. Brown was an ex-officer, a really good man, but with no sense of humour. The History master spent half his time writing letters to his girl-friends, which gave us all great enjoyment.

"By the way, one of the boys at school, who often walked home with me, was truly a future celebrity – Rabbi Schonfeld, son of a rabbi, who later pioneered a Jewish School, and who, even as a youngster was truly brilliant. I was really proud of his achievements."

I asked Harry about Life in London during the Twenties, particularly from the viewpoint of a young Jewish lad. He says: "Around 1922 anti-semitism was never far away, but not at the school, and I'm pleased to say this goes for today (2004) as well, but we will always have to live with it."

Writing in capital letters, he adds: "It will be remarkable if you can read my handwriting, my typewriter broke down forty-three years ago, and I might sue the Manufacturers!"

I had asked in my letter, whether to end with "Yours truly" or with "Mazzeltoff!" He ended his letter: "Mazzeltoff! is quite in order, because in the past year I have become a great grandfather twice."

# Chapter Two
# *What Highburians did in the War*

Many old Highbury County alumni did of course "do their bit," and several of them made the ultimate sacrifice. On 27 December 1940 the *Islington Gazette* reported that "a very prominent sportsman among the Old Boys of Highbury County School, "Bill" Meredith had died in hospital recently from wounds received in France. Also reported in that issue was: "One Old Boy, Sergeant H. Davis has been awarded the Distinguished Flying Cross."

A "Book of Remembrance" commemorated them in our time. This had been produced in a lavish copperplate hand, probably by the Art Department, and was housed in a glazed-top wooden case on a plinth, reputedly crafted by the late Mr. Lindsey Lane, the woodwork master. This always stood in a corner of the assembly hall. Sadly, all enquiries as to its whereabouts have proved fruitless. To paraphrase the official language of their time, The Book of Remembrance is "missing, presumed destroyed."

## A Cloak & Dagger War

On 3 September 1939 war was declared with Germany and shortly afterwards Alfred Arthur Wright, then aged 23, found himself in the army.

Alf Wright was in SOE (the Special Operations Executive) where he was attached to the French Section, working with the French Resistance, at Grendon Underwood. He was a wireless telegraphist, who instructed agents in ciphered transmission and decoding. Among his "pupils" were Violette Szabo, whose story was told in the book, *Carve Her Name With Pride*, made into a film starring Virginia McKenna in the 1950s; also Denise Block, both of whom, together with another member of FANY (Field Auxiliary Nursing Yeomanry), were killed in Ravensbruck concentration camp.

Alf writes: "I do not favour either the French or the German nation. I can tell you that any Frenchman could get £100 for denouncing a British Agent. I would rather not tell you about "Odette" Sansom, who managed to convince her interrogators that she and Captain Peter Churchill, with whom she had been captured, were related to Winston Churchill, and might therefore be more use to the Germans as hostages, than as corpses. Controversially, this ploy was later seen by some as saving her own skin, at the expense of her comrades.

"The secrecy of SOE was poor," Alf continued, "Some agents, feeling fed-up, gathered together in a restaurant somewhere in France, speaking in English!

They were worth £100 each! At our end agents who were captured, either gave an incorrect code, or were supposed to omit a code-word, to show that they had been captured. At this time the German military Intelligence (*Abwehr*) had seriously compromised SOE's Dutch Section. Well, some operators at this end replied to such distress signals by answering "Thank you, but please give your correct code number in future!"

Alf continued: "At that time you worked in your Section, and were prevented from contact with any other foreign Section. At Grendon Underwood I was attached to the French Section and nothing else. The only exception I remember was a "FANY" called Yvonne Basille, whom I met at Tring." Years afterwards, he met an MI6 officer at Bletchley Park, who showed him the same type of encoder which he had used during the war. The officer reminded him that he was still subject to the Official Secrets Act.

## The Beverton Tapes

Ronald Beverton was 15 or 16 when war broke out in 1939. He was evacuated to Chippenham, Wiltshire, where he was to spend an uneasy eighteen months. The families who would take in younger evacuee children would not consider a teenage lad, whom they felt should be working for his living. From the start, Ronald's sole aim was to get into University and become a teacher. Even when Ronald's father offered an extra five shillings per week, it was felt that he would be too expensive to keep. He eventually found lodgings, but there were no facilities for him to study, so Ronald was forced to get on his bicycle and ride into the countryside or to the park with his books. Then he discovered public reading rooms that were open in the evenings and at weekends, where he could study in peace. He left school in 1942 after he had gained his Higher Schools examination, applied and in autumn 1942 he was accepted for a place reading German & English at Bristol University.

As Ronald said, he had "barely got his feet under the table at University" when he became 18 in December 1942 and his call-up papers arrived. At the suggestion of the Dean of Bristol University, his German professor, Ron applied to join the Inter-Services Languages School, a department of military counter-intelligence, MI6. He was accepted, given the rank of corporal, and joined nine other candidates on a course in written and oral Japanese and Japanese culture.

Posted initially to the Duke of York's Barracks in Chelsea, London, he spent the next eighteen months learning Japanese as well as other skills such as how to drive motor cycles, cars and various kinds of military vehicles. Next came what was called "sleuthing', or how to follow people while remaining undetected. Then came a three-day spell at "Station "X"" at Bletchley Park, where he learned microphotography, encoding, deciphering, clandestine wireless transmission, and other covert surveillance methods.

In October 1944 he was one of three from his course selected to join the Government Communications Bureau, where he translated captured intelligence documents for MI6.

In January 1945, after eighteen months' learning to speak and read Japanese, and still with the rank of only a corporal, Ronald was posted to 103 Special Intelligence Unit at Supreme Headquarters Allied Forces in Europe, (SHAFE) in Brussels. Transport arrangements were still chaotic at this time, and he had to make his own way, "hitching a lift" across the Channel to Calais, thence to a Red Cross Transit Camp, where conditions were abysmal until a sympathetic officer offered Ron a camp bed in his own quarters. The following day he was able to catch a train from Calais to Brussels. His work was to translate documents. Although quartered in a comfortable apartment in the centre of Brussels, Ron became frustrated with his lot, and persuaded his Intelligence Corps C.O. to recommend him for Officer Training, and he returned to an Officer Training Unit in Yorkshire.

In May 1945 Ronald passed the War Office Selection Board (WOSB) to be commissioned Second Lieutenant. He saved some of the £50 allowance for fitting himself out as an officer, by buying a second hand uniform, formerly the property of a Captain. This made it look as if he had been demoted to Second Lieutenant, but he says, " I could afford a bottle of wine with dinner, out of the change!" He was then posted to First Canadian Division HQ at Tilberg in Holland, where he experienced a couple of near misses from German V1 missiles being fired from the Eastern side of the Rhine against the advancing Allied forces. These missiles would sometimes malfunction, and on two occasions landed within the HQ perimeter, causing damage and some casualties. After a few weeks he was recalled to Brussels and then to an internment centre for German refugees in London, where he was involved as a translator in screening the genuine refugees for possible fugitive Nazis.

The war ended in August 1945 while he was still in London awaiting an overseas posting to the Far East. This arrived in September, when he embarked on a three-day flight to South East Asia Command (SEAC), Colombo, in Ceylon (now Sri Lanka). After a spell there translating captured Japanese documents, he was moved on to Bangkok in Siam (Thailand). His work there was in vetting Japanese prisoners of war and suspected sympathisers, which introduced a more political element into the work. It was during this period, as Ronald recounted on tape, that he came into contact with a sort of Mata Hari character; an extremely attractive Anglo-Asian woman who, it was suspected, had enjoyed liaisons with both Japanese and Allied officers, and had been acting as a double agent. British Counter-Intelligence wanted to investigate her activities more closely, and perhaps "turn" her into spying for our side. Unfortunately, while she was interned in an allegedly "secure" compound awaiting interrogation, she seduced an Indian guard and made good her escape.

Ron Beverton's "Cloak & Dagger" career concluded with a posting to Intelligence G2 in Singapore early in 1946, where he soon found that the Intelligence work was being scaled down. Colleagues in the South African forces were being posted home and released. By now he was impatient to return to University, so in July 1946 he applied for a "Class B" demobilisation so that he could resume his studies. This was duly granted, and Ron was flown home in August 1946 in time to return to Bristol University that autumn.

*   *   *   *   *

Ken Bass became 18 in July 1945. National Service was imminent, but he was not called up until February 1946. Most of his military service was spent as an Assistant Technical Instructor, with the rank of sergeant in the Royal Army Ordnance Corps in front of a blackboard, teaching reluctant recruits to become clerks and storemen. Towards the end of his service however, he had a lively and interesting six months when he was posted to a Special Stores Unit, attached to 2nd Independent Parachute Brigade. When demobilisation came due, Ken resisted the temptations to continue with army life, and returned home in August 1948.

*   *   *   *   *

David Nelson started at Highbury County in 1944, just after the school had reopened. He told us that during the wartime, "Boggy" Marsh kept the boys in school during the lunchtime break. Weary of this restriction, he and a friend one day escaped to Highbury Fields to play football. While they were kicking the ball around, a V1 Flying Bomb came droning over; suddenly its motor cut out. At that time, everyone knew that this meant the bomb was about to drop to the ground and explode. So David and his pal started running for shelter – not back to school but towards the public toilets behind Highbury Underground station, which in their confusion they thought would offer some protection.

The bomb landed in the front area of the last but one fine Georgian house in Compton Terrace, on the other side of Highbury Corner, killing 20 people and injuring many more. The branch of Barclays Bank next to the station, two houses nearby, and five houses in Compton Terrace itself were all destroyed.

David and his pal had fortunately changed direction and sheltered in the doorway of one of the houses in Highbury Place, where apart from being showered with debris they were unhurt. On the way back to school, they ran into "Boggy" who, on learning of their close shave, "went crazy", says David.

## Chapter Three
# Down Memory Lane to Highbury Grove

*Oft in the stilly night,*
*'Ere Slumber's chain has bound me,*
*Fond Memory brings the light*
*Of other days around me.*
　　　　　Thomas Moore, *National Airs* (1815)

W e find ourselves in Highbury Grove at the site of our *alma mater*. Sadly
now only two brick gateposts and the old Gymnasium building remain
as vestiges of Highbury County School. We would now beg of the reader "that
willing suspension of disbelief, for the moment, which constitutes poetic faith,"
as Samuel Taylor Coleridge puts it.

Imagine now before us stands once more that imposing three-storey edifice
of brick and Portland stone built as a children's home in 1853. Walk between
the brick posts and approach the imposing main entrance porch, mount the
stone steps to the main front door. In the few surviving photographs, the building
is depicted as probably most of us remember it; the brickwork begrimed from
its exposure for over a hundred years to London's soot-laden atmosphere,
derived not only from the nearby railways, but also from the coal fires used in
every home and industry. How much more imposing might the School building
have appeared, had it survived to be cleaned and restored, as have so many
other public buildings in more recent times.

In those days of long ago only the staff, sixth formers, and unfortunate late-
comers were allowed to enter this way, where names were entered in the "Late
Book," along with a reason for one's lateness! In our imagination however, we
may walk confidently past the Staff Room on our left, and the Headmaster's
Study to our right, to pause for a moment before the niche on the wall facing
us. Here hung the school clock, and below it the bell push, by which the lesson
periods and break-times were regulated.

To the right, stone stairs lead upwards but again only the privileged are
allowed to ascend this way. To the left a short corridor leads forwards towards
the Assembly Hall. At precisely one minute to nine o'clock on every school
morning, the Headmaster left his study to pass this way, gown flowing behind
him, to take Morning Assembly. In the Hall the boys stood in rows according
to seniority. First-years in front, nearest the proscenium, while the seniors are
ranged further back, with a few Sixth formers propping up the far wall.

Surveying all on the left of the platform stood the tall ramrod straight figure of Latin Master "Leo" Lincoln, with iron-grey hair, in dark suit and academic gown, watchful but impassive, ignoring the babble arising from the throng. At the same moment as the Headmaster left his study, "Leo" would take up position at centre stage, without a word. Woe betides the lad who failed to heed the unspoken command for silence. One remembers to this day the feeling of those gimlet eyes boring into the back of one's head, as the realisation dawns that everyone else has fallen silent!

The Headmaster arrived, a number of prefects would take post along the back of the stage, and Morning Assembly began. Mr. Lincoln took his place at the piano, hymns were sung – the School Hymn perhaps, "Who would true valour see," adapted from John Bunyan's *The Pilgrim's Progress*. The Head read the prayers, and announced any significant events in the life of the school. A prayer would be said and the Assembly was dismissed form by form to disperse to their form-rooms where lessons began; "'Oh dear, double period Maths!!" Jewish boys and staff members had their own morning worship, held usually in the school library, along the corridor from the entrance lobby.

Opposite the Hall doors is a hatchway concealing a dumb-waiter lift-shaft connecting with the school kitchens in the basement, ordinarily reached by the stairway to the left of the liftshaft. If we descend here we find ourselves in a similar short corridor to that on the ground floor, running from front to back of the building. To the front several storerooms opened off the corridor; these are said to have been used as confinement cells for malefactors in the days when the truant school was here. Turn to our right, however, and we pass the kitchens where the school dinners for about 200 boys were prepared daily. Opposite the kitchen the corridor turns sharply right. The next door on our right was the study of Revd. E.G. Taylor, Religious Instruction master. He also ran the school choir and organised the Summer Camps at Seaton in Devon. Outside this underground office, the corridor leads out into a sunken underpass, which connects the north and south playgrounds, protected by wrought-iron railings.

A flight of stone steps leads up from the underpass to ground level and the old Gymnasium, strangely spared from demolition in 1967. It is a rectangular building, presenting its long elevation to us, with tall windows and a mansard roof, provided with skylights. The entrance is at the end nearest to us. Within, a screened off area provides a changing room, lined with coat hooks. Beyond this is the highly polished and sprung wooden floor. Woe betides the boy who enters without first removing his street shoes! The long wall on our left is furnished with wall-bars, up and down which we seemed condemned forever to climb – for no other purpose for their use was ever explained to us! Wooden gymnastic beams hung by rope and pulley from the ceiling, as did the climbing ropes. In the far corners were stored the wooden horse and the vaulting horse, while tumbling mats and other paraphernalia had each its allotted place.

*Highbury County School in the 1930s*
*(Photo: Islington Local History Centre, Islington Libaries)*

We leave the Gym to return to the main building. Beneath a lean-to cover were to be found the outdoor toilets. No lingering here in the winter! A few steps up from here, a door leads into the indoor wash rooms, with hot and cold running water, and a cloak-room. Now we find ourselves back in the corridor outside the Hall.

A turn to our left takes us through to the front of the building, where another turn in the corridor brings us back to a classroom – perhaps even our form room. Our next lesson may be Biology, so grabbing the necessary books from our desks, we hurry along the corridor to the staircase at the end of the building, and ascend two floors to the top floor.

On the first floor landing a storeroom on the left has been turned over to a common room for the Arts Sixth. Next to that lies one of the senior form rooms. Hurrying on to our right, for the period bell has sounded again, brings us to the Biology Laboratory. Was there always a partially dissected rabbit on display there, for so it seemed?

When at length the bell signals the end of the lesson and break time, we stream back down the corridor, down the staircase and return our books to our desks. Back along the corridor past the Hall, down some stone steps out into the junior playground. This north playground is enclosed by a curtain wall in which a double gateway furnished with stone copings atop twin brick gateposts gives on to the driveway and Highbury Grove.

At the inner end of this area stood a plain four-square brick building, with an external iron staircase giving access to the Art Room on the first floor. A fate worse than death awaited the unwary boy who was surprised here by the Art master in the storeroom, or so legend had it at the time!

On the ground floor was the woodwork workshop, where many "face-sides" were "planed flat and smooth," tenons were sawn and chiselled, under the supervision of the late Mr. Lindsey Lane. As he passed the bench where I was struggling through some exercise, he picked up a chisel from the rack on the end of the bench. Holding the tool by the point, he held it in front of me.

"Which end is the handle?" he asked.

"There Sir!" I pointed out correctly.

"Just wanted to make sure you knew," he replied tartly.

Across the playground facing the craft workshops was the indoor swimming pool, which must have held the coldest water outside the Arctic Ocean.

So back to our form-room for another change of books, and off to the Physics Laboratory, where a permanently sun tanned "Sam" Golding enlightened us to the Laws of Physics. Just in time, there goes the bell to end the day. Return past the washrooms. Up the steps into the front corridor.

Before we dash away, though, let us ascend the central staircase to visit the school secretary's office on the first floor landing. In the corridor opposite, accommodation had been provided for the Caretaker, Mr. Percy Clavey and his family, when the school-keeper's house in Highbury New Park had been commandeered for emergency housing during the War.

One floor up to the top floor corridor, to discover the narrow stairway entrance to the attic rooms, which were for a time used as a common room by the science sixth formers.

We have walked quietly around the School from bottom to top, and end to end. The final bell has sounded, so we now cross the senior playground, passing the Gym, to leave by the wicket gate on to Highbury New Park.

The brown brick edifice of the Telephone Exchange, and opposite on the corner of Highbury New Park, the 1930s built block of flats remain as most of us knew them. Still standing too, is the pub "The Alwyne Arms," where in days of yore "Charlie" Garrett, and other staff used to enjoy a lunch-time pint. In those days the pub comprised both public and saloon bars, arranged in a horseshoe. Unfortunately some Fifth formers of my acquaintance were enjoying an illicit beer in the Public bar, when they found themselves face-to-face with the said History master, across the bar in the Saloon bar!

Leaving the "Alwyne Arms', I return to Highbury New Park, there to await the single-deck bus on route 236 to Stroud Green. At other times we would walk along St. Paul's Road towards Highbury Corner to the bus stop. From

*Above and below: the old Gymnasium which survived the establishment of Highbury Grove School and is now used for community activities. — Photographs by Old Highburian, R.E. (Bobby) Bartram.*

here my route home was by trolleybus, route 609 or 611 to Nags Head, then any bus to Finsbury Park. Perhaps your route takes you on foot from Highbury Corner through to the "Bill-dins" in Liverpool Road or through the back lanes of Canonbury to Essex Road or to the Angel.

# Chapter Four
# *In and out of the Staff Room*

In July 1953, a group photograph of the staff was taken in the north playground. The occasion was the retirement of Mr. R.J. Marsh, after 25 years as Headmaster. It was also a chance for some of the younger members of staff to survey their older colleagues and sum up the spirit of Highbury County.

The staff photograph is reproduced on the page opposite, having been kindly lent by Dennis Lewis, who taught Maths and football. On this page and those following are character sketches of this fascinating group of educationalists taken from: (RB) the contemporary diary of Ronald Beverton, who had joined the staff in September 1950 to teach German; (GC) notes by George Cobby, who became Second French Master in 1949 (incidentally, it was the first teaching post for both Ron and George); (GJ) reminiscences of the fifties by Geoff Jones; and (DP) additional notes by David Perman.

**Brian Youngs**, age 29 (in July 1953). Teaches Biology.
(RB) Plays badminton and tennis, but has a distinct predilection for the latter. Extremely sociable and gregarious, he has a lot to say about most topics, and has an infectious laugh. He has become a close friend. Extremely free and uninhibited, but cannot abide cigarettes.

(DP) Brian Youngs is still with us, looking much the same today aged 80 as he does in the school photograph. He still practises his other skill (than teaching) as an osteopath. And he is still "extremely sociable and gregarious".

**George Cobby**, age 27. Second French master.
(RB) Rather tied up with his work, at the expense of outside activities. Sensitive and at times aggressive, he has a deep, full-throated voice, and a flair for humorous mimicry, together with a biting, caustic wit. Engaged to Patricia Poulten, school secretary.

(DP) Again, a Highbury master who has worn well. There is an appreciation of George in the next chapter and his views on a variety of topics in the following chapter: "Confessions of the Beaks". George Cobby, who lives in Little Chalfont where he enjoys pottering in his garden and listening to classical music, is the diligent and sociable President of the present Old Highburians Association.

Back row: *B.K.Youngs (Biology), G.W.H.Cobby (French), C.F.Winter (Maths), L.Gillespie (English), R.J.Beverton (German), A.E.Rosenthal (French).*

Centre row: *L.G.Davies (Geography), W.H.Laurie (Art), E.S.Wood (English & Careers), E.G.Taylor (Divinity), J.M.Knowles (History etc), L.E.Lane (Handicraft), J.H.Duffield (Junior Science), D.Lewis (Maths).*

Front row (seated): *Miss P. Poulten (Secretary), S.B.Davis (Chemistry), V.F. Gage (Games & PT), C.J.K.Garrett (History), P.I.Howells (Second Master & French), R.J. Marsh (Head), S.E.Golding (Physics), L.H.L.Lincoln (Latin), A.P.Chapman (Maths), D.C.Leech (English), Mrs.D.Gauld (Music).*

**Colin Winter**, age 28, teaches Maths.

(RB) He is dour, correct and careful in his attitudes in and out of school, but often unconventional in his thought. Has a philosophical bent and acts only after much premeditation. He plays badminton, is an active rugger player, and school athletic coach. He is likeable, but sometimes unapproachable.

**Leslie Gillespie**, age 32, teaches English.

(RB) He is witty, rueful, with a soft and undulating voice; tells a good story, full of Irish blarney. He dislikes teaching and longs to be free from such bourgeois impediments of time & place. Hates Leech. Seems to drift and dream through life. I like him.

**Ronald Beverton**, age 29, teaches German.

(DP) Ron Beverton did not comment on his own character in this part of his diary, but material about his life and thought appears as an "appreciation" in the next chapter.

**Adolf Ernest Rosenthal** ('Rosie') about 40, teaches French.

(RB) He still has a thick German accent, although he left that country in the '30s. He is restless, excitable and liable to fly off at a tangent, which amuses boys and staff alike. Vociferous in his likes and dislikes. Unconventional dress. Talks a lot, as university professors tend to do.

(GC) Ernest Rosenthal became a great friend. Most boys knew of the mishaps and misfortunes that befell him from the moment the Gestapo poisoned his Alsatian dogs. It is a little-known fact that he turned down the chance of a wealthy lifestyle in America, because of his devotion to the country which had given him shelter. This was exceeded only by his passion for justice, which he did not always receive himself. Rosie's classroom discipline was famous, and his self-discipline often led him into extraordinary situations. He could be a kind of poor man's James Bond (without the bimbos) and a few of his escapades were worthy of P.G. Wodehouse, as when during the Coronation celebrations, he recovered several hundred pairs of opera glasses missing from Sadlers Wells Theatre, the teenage audience having mistakenly believed that sixpence in the slot entitled them to ownership of the said optical instruments. Rosie's discipline was never more justified than by an incident which occurred after he had left Highbury. He was leading a school excursion out of Calais when a car crashed into the coach. The two vehicles swerved into an electricity pylon and burst into flames. The car's six occupants were killed outright. Rosie was catapulted through the coach windscreen, got back on and rescued his forty boys in as many seconds. He then got the party back to Calais and on the first available ferry before the authorities had finished their elevenses. Teachers don't come like Rosie any more.

(GJ) Mr. Rosenthal, a refugee from Czechoslovakia, taught us the most perfect French, I'm sure. However when he became excited his English diction became somewhat less than clear, and his mixed metaphors became legend. Made angry by one pupil, who left himself wide open, the master shouted heatedly, " If ze cap fits upon ze shoes, vare zem!" (sic) We wondered what the prefects, who monitored compliance with the correct wearing of school uniform at the gates, would have had to say about this unsuitable treatment of a school-cap!

This miscreant was luckier than most, however. Mr. Rosenthal had devised a most excruciating means, by which to punish and humiliate those of his pupils who became too cheeky. He would stand close to the offender, many of whom were taller than himself, and take the short hairs of their side-burn between his thumb and index-finger. He would then simply raise his hand, lifting his hapless prey to their feet, and even to their tiptoes, if he were severely displeased with them! Not even the toughest youngster could withstand this approach. It was most effective, and left no marks!

**Len Davies**, age 40-ish, teaches Geography.

(RB) A very affable Welshman, who intended to enter Law, and now talks like a lawyer, discursive, detailed and digressive. He is conventional but pleasant, sociable and paternal in his approach to other staff members. Likes to feel he's one of the lads.

(GC) One who could brighten the darkest day with a quip was Davies the Map, who initiated me into the pleasures and perils of school outings. With Welsh relish he would regale us with woeful tales of always losing his way on army manoeuvres and I have often wondered whether that was why he inspired his classes to draw such immaculate maps.

**Bill Laurie** age about 32, teaches Art.

(RB) He is softly spoken, temperamental, busy and retiring, colourful in dress and action. He tends to be conventional in his arguments; grumbles about impositions on his time. Popular with the boys (sic). Generally likeable.

(DP) Bill Laurie was a good painter and exhibited in the Royal Academy Summer Exhibition. He was a conscientious objector and served in the National Fire Service in the war.

**E.S. (Stanley) Wood**, age 45, teaches English.

(RB) Conventional and precise, he talks only when he has something to say. He works hard, and can be opinionated and humourless at times in speech, but is amusing when "offstage".

(GC) Stan Wood was quietly and marvellously supportive, one of the "backbones of the staff".

(GJ) Mr. Wood taught English throughout the School. He regularly carried a copy of *The Spectator* which he encouraged us to read, and from which he liked to quote, so as to "open up" our minds. He was often drawn into "Red

Herring" discussions. At one stage, several of us were encouraged regularly to pay out our pennies for copies on issue day.

(DP) Mr. Wood was my form master in the first and fifth years and, in contrast to the partisan Donald Leech, had a balanced and catholic view of English Literature. With his wife and two daughters, ably assisted by Mr. Lane and his family, he ran one of the school's agricultural camps at Williton in Somerset. In 1965, on Mr. King's retirement, he became Acting Head and in 1967 the deputy to Rhodes Boyson in the new Highbury Grove Comprehensive School.

**Reverend E.G. Taylor**, age about 55, teaches R.I.

(RB) Affectionately known as "the Bishop." Although rarely seen in the staff room, he is kindly, his voice is rich & sonorous, as well toned as his figure is well covered. He is very sympathetic to the boys and runs the school camp regularly in summer and the choir in winter.

(GJ) In his lapel "E.G." wore the emblem of the Old Contemptibles, denoting that he had served with the British Expeditionary Force in France at the start of WWI. He was a colossus of a man, and was unique in the culture of the school. He presided over his domain in his study, tucked away in the basement, its walls lined with obscure tomes, which overflowed the shelves, in piles all round the room. If you happened to belong to the school choir, as I did, one had frequent access there. For after every school concert at Easter and Christmas, the whole choir was invited into the great man's den, there to indulge in great platefuls of jelly and blancmange; a welcome reward for having sung oneself hoarse. To face that conductor's grizzly visage, with all its passion, joy, imploring soulfulness and humour continually forming and evaporating before your very eyes; in league with those great hands, desperately clawing notes, sounds and silences from the choir, the ether, the angels or wherever they could be obtained, is something that will remain with me forever.

(DP) As Geoff Jones says, Edward Goodrham Taylor was unique in the culture of Highbury, and possibly of any school. His energy in all he did – teaching Divinity throughout the school, running the choir for two full-scale concerts and a church service as well as organising school camps at Seaton – was no better illustrated than in his vigorous conducting. Geoff is right about the "grizzly visage": E.G. was a bear of a man. He was a stretcher-bearer in the First World War, like one of his heroes, Ralph Vaughan-Williams. He studied history at Leeds, then theology at Westcott House, Cambridge, inspired to the ministry by the suffering and courage he had witnessed in Flanders. Stoddart-Kennedy ("Woodbine Willy") was one of his favourite poets. But he was determinedly liberal in his theology: as I was intending to be ordained at that time, E.G. introduced me to *The Quest for the Historical Jesus* by Albert

Schweitzer (another hero). I remember a class in the Remove, when E.G. was describing the sand banks in the Sea of Galilee which (he said) went a long way to explaining Jesus "walking on the water", when a large lad in front of me remarked: "Ere, couldn't it 'ave just bin a miracle?" E.G. had a great affection for machinery. At school camps, he loaded all sorts of equipment, particularly Primus stoves, into the back and trunk of his large Morris sedan, and he operated a 12" gauge model railway when staying with his brother in Bovey Tracey on the edge of Dartmoor. There is a charming and sympathetic portrait of E.G. in Zvi Jagendorf's novel *Wolfy and the Strudelbakers* (Dewi Lewis Publishing). A remarkable man!

**Max ('Nobby') Knowles**, aged 38, teaches Junior History, English & Maths.

(RB) He is an active Liberal in Watford. In his work he is retiring and assiduous. While softly spoken, he is easily irritated, but very pleasant in his outbursts of ribald humour.

(GC) Max Knowles was another (with Philip Howells) who showed me what it was to be a schoolmaster and not just a teacher. He was often thought of as a man who ran school dinners. He did that supremely well, too. In my early days I had the good fortune to teach his classes and was able to learn from him what it was to be a good form-teacher. In that capacity I have never met his equal since. He was a fine organiser, and working with him, inside or outside the classroom, you always knew what was expected of you, and always knew that you could and would do it.

**Lindsey Lane**, age 37, teaches woodwork.

(RB) He is reticent, though sometimes outspokenly opinionated, but easily embarrassed. An acolyte of Donald Leech, he attaches himself to the bridge table like a limpet.

**Jim Duffield**, age 36, Junior Science teacher.

(RB) An unsympathetic left-winger from Cumberland, he is not popular with some of the other staff; and is a regular participant in the Lunchtime Bridge group.

(DP) The only sex lessons I had at Highbury were from Mr. Duffield. But I don't remember him telling us anything

about the sexual act (which remained a mystery for some years afterwards); he was solely concerned with the differences between gonorrhoea and syphilis.

**Dennis Lewis**, age 28, teaches Maths and football.

(RB) He is very friendly and sociable, even generous, but tends to compensate for his basic shyness by being over talkative. He loves football, but dislikes Gage (PT. & Games). He plays badminton, and gives up a lot of his time after school to coaching.

**Patricia Poulten**, age 25, School secretary.

(RB) Charming! Engaged to George Cobby.

(DP) They were married the same year and she remained School Secretary until 1961. There is more about Mrs. Cobby in the appreciation of her husband in the next chapter. Sadly she died in 1997.

**Steve Davis**, age 49, teaches Chemistry.

(RB) Good natured, friendly and retiring. Neutral.

(GC) Steve Davis (with Stan Wood) was quietly and marvellously supportive and one of the two backbones of the staff. Steve rarely spoke in staffroom meetings, but was an exceptionally perceptive observer of what was going on.

He also ran a film club, with some very well chosen movies. It was amazing that our rackety old building could house a "cinema". I found it equally surprising that this lovely quiet man adored horse-racing and was an ardent fan of the Marx Brothers.

**Vivian Gage**, age 54, teaches PT & Games.

(RB) Unpopular with all.

(DP) A sadist!

**Edmund ('Eddie') Garrett**, age 55, teaches History.

(RB) Friendly and amusing, although somewhat brusque. Loves his beer!

(GC) "Charlie" Garrett was the supreme character of the staffroom. His real name was Edmund ("My Old Thing" to his wife) and was addressed as Eddie by only one or two of his contemporaries. The others called him by his surname, the rest of us added 'Mr.' as we did for all our seniors. He always sat in the same place.

**Phillip Howells**, age 59: Senior Master teaches French.

(RB) Jovial, always jesting and boisterous. Due for retirement next year, his interest in teaching is waning.

(GC) The first person you could always rely on was Philip Howells, deputy head and my head of department. He was the linchpin of the school, and in my experience no one has ever come within light years of his ability to simplify organisation and to inspire confidence in all who worked with him. He was scrupulously fair: if you said or did something stupid, you could be sure of a sharp rebuke, and this applied equally to his contemporaries as to new men. On occasions of staff shortages, he had been known to supervise three classes simultaneously, rather than call unfairly (as he saw it) on others. His secret was his untiring energy and his acceptance of one hundred per cent responsibility for his job. I have known others in his position who would run a mile rather than do that.

**Robert (R.J.) Marsh**, age 60, Headmaster (or "Boggy" to everyone)

(RB) The most misliked and mistrusted member of staff because of his narrow-sighted and hypercritical attitude to life. He suffers from sugar diabetes, which may influence his perception of life. He punches the Bible from the platform in school assembly every morning, and stresses the Christian

way of life, but does not always live up to it himself. Most of the staff regard him as weak. He is sentimental, and voices certain inferiority. His passivity alternates with outbursts of extreme fury, when he will shout unrestrainedly. He is mean to the extent of saving pennies on food. It is common knowledge that during his dinner duty, (which brings the perk of a free meal to all those who do it), he collects uneaten scraps of meat from the boys' plates in a tin which he conceals beneath his gown. These he takes home to feed his chickens! Every afternoon at four he scrounges a free cup of tea, for which the staff have paid, from the staff room. At some time or other he infuriates almost everybody – except "Rosie" who has only praise for him.

(GJ) A further privilege which being part of the school choir brought was awarded by that other great Christian gentleman of the school, the head himself, Mr. R.J. Marsh, who was also a member. Each term, in recognition of the amount of after hours time we gave up to practice, we were allowed an extra half day's holiday.

(DP) A very different assessment of Mr. Marsh from Beverton's is given on page 42. As editor of *The Highburian Magazine* in 1953, I commissioned it from Mr. Lincoln who was diplomacy itself. Anyway, Boggy himself read it.

**Sam Golding**, age about 55, teaches physics.

(RB) Boggy's keenest enemy! Usually rather shy and silent, except when on a pet theme (amongst which "Boggy" features prominently). Despite his formal outlook on life, and reactionary tendencies, he is very pleasant and an avid tennis player. He has no time for modern progressive elements in education.

**Leslie Lincoln**, age about 55, teaches Latin.

(RB) Very shy, he is reserved and sensitive, and only has eyes for his own subject – and photography, of which he produces some excellent examples. He is interested in silent reading and music, not so silent. He says he's a liberal or a socialist, but acts like a conservative. He plays with the Bridge group and frequently loses his temper and sulks.

(GC) At the opposite pole from other members of staff, at least externally, was Les Lincoln, who rarely said a word but, when he did, it was really worth hearing. His apparent sternness disguised a man of great warmth and humour.

(DP) I certainly endorse George Cobby's judgement. Mr. Lincoln was the most fascinating man in the school and I am sure I got my place at Oxford by doing a pen portrait of him in my college entrance exam. For one thing, he dressed in striped trousers and dark waistcoat and jacket (like a Victorian bank clerk) but also wore spats and hobnail boots. You could see these when he played the piano in Assembly. He was a fine musician and would play records to the Assembly while we waited for Marsh – I particularly remember Sibelius's *Swan of Tuonela*. Though reserved with other members of staff and younger boys who feared him, Lincoln was unbuttoned (not literally!) with the Sixth Form. Here he would smoke his foul, saltpetre-less cigarettes, instruct us in the delights of Virgil and Horace, with the addition of the occasional ribaldry. It was from Lincoln I learned the famous limerick which finishes: "Who did what and what with and to whom?"

**A. P. Chapman**, age about 49, Senior Maths master.

(RB) Naturally retiring, but often astonishingly exuberant, he talks freely when interested and shows complete lack of reserve. He has an amazing head for figures, and can remember the examination marks of boys going back years!

He is full of the most audacious curiosity, and always asks with a direct question, more often than not completely unconnected with the immediate conversation. Admits to a conservative – liberal bias. He is practical, mean and calculating, and lends only if he can be certain of getting it back. Cadges lifts. He is interested in all kinds of sport, particularly tennis and rugby.

(DP) Chapman was a charming man, interested in phrenology which led him to handle the foreheads of younger boys while pronouncing on their futures. His colleague in the Maths Department, Dennis Lewis, said Chapman was always courteous and always supportive. I remember him for his lyric tenor voice and the solos he sang at carol concerts, particularly Pretorius's "Three Kings from Persian Lands Afar"

**Donald Leech**, age 51, Senior English master.

(RB) He is conceited and forceful, & loud in dress as well as voice; rude, sensitive, and aggressive. He overwhelms in argument by sheer volume of voice, and intimidates by braggadocio gestures. He is an inveterate Bridge player with boundless energy who irritates everybody.

(DP) Leech was ruled by his Super-ego. He was the supremely confident producer of the Highbury Dramatic Society plays of the '50s, bellowing his commands at all and sundry. I appeared in four of them but only after he had literally beaten my Cockney vowels into the shape he required. Outside school, his life also revolved around amateur dramatics. Away from the classroom he chain-smoked Senior Service. As Senior English master, he was totally in love with the Romantics, telling us that Dryden and Pope wrote disguised prose.

**Mrs. M. Gauld**, age 53, teaches music at the school three days each week.

(RB) Although she has served here 12 years, as the only female staff member she is retiring and quietly mannered. No one seems to know her very well.

(GC) Mrs. Gauld became the Music teacher in 1943 and continued throughout the fifties era. She died in either 1999 or 2000, aged 100, having received her telegram from the Queen.

(DP) A charming lady but not a terribly effective teacher. It was her fate to be the only female outside their families that most Highbury boys met. She was thus both a matronly, mother figure and also the subject of countless juvenile fantasies. On one occasion (I cannot remember what we had done wrong) she sent me and another boy to stand outside the Head's study – not usually much of a punishment because you could escape when the bell rang for the next lesson. Unfortunately, on that occasion Marsh appeared and beckoned us into his study. "You know, boys," he said, creasing his fat cheeks in what he assumed was a smile, "you really must not rub Mrs. Gauld up the wrong way." At that, we fell about in fits of laughter and were promptly caned on the spot.

## Mr. R.J. Marsh – an Appreciation

It was in 1928 that Mr. Marsh came as Headmaster to Highbury from Sheffield and of his earlier life I know little except that he was a Shropshire man and had been, before going to Sheffield, on the staff of one of our Public Schools, Worksop College. In many ways it was a difficult move for him, for he was quite unused to the London boy and to the mixed social strata from which Highbury necessarily drew its pupils. His first year or so here was for him a period of difficult adjustment, but one over which he triumphed magnificently by his determination and the quality of his character. He reorganised the school and laid the foundations upon which the Sixth Form was built.

The amount of work he put in during those early days was prodigious; he formed personal contacts with the Heads of Primary Schools, seeking and succeeding in attracting to Highbury the best of their scholarship boys; by personal contact with parents he induced those whose boys had failed to pass the scholarship examination to send their boys to Highbury as fee-payers and then spent long hours after school coaching them for the supplementary examination at the age of 13, one result of which was that in 1932 the school gained more Supplementary Junior Scholarships than any other school in London. In these ways he not only raised the numbers in the school from 320 to 540 but vastly improved the intellectual standard, making possible the university successes which, in due course, followed. It is true, I think, to say that the foundation laid and built by Mr. Marsh from 1929 to the War gave his staff the material and provided them with the opportunity to compete successfully in university and State Scholarships open to any school in the country.

Yet it was not just the school or its reputation that mattered to him; in a real sense he carried the boys in his heart. It must be remembered that these were years of depression and unemployment, and so he drove the boys hard for their own sakes, and when the time came for them to leave he was unsatisfied until all of them were placed. In these days of full employment we find it hard to understand why the School Magazine of December, 1934, should record with such satisfaction that 18 out of 21 boys, who had left with matriculation the previous June, had found employment. Behind all these efforts for the intellectual and social welfare of the boys lay a deeper interest: each boy was for him the child of God.

One of his first actions on coming to the school was to adopt Bunyan's Pilgrim Song as the School Hymn, and, on 11 March 1934, there began a series of School Services which, although voluntary, have always been well attended and it was with the sense that they were missing something of vital importance, that he grieved when some held themselves aloof. This conviction was born of his own experience, for he was a man of deep religious faith and at no time did he fail in his Prize Day Speech to urge upon parents their fundamental duty, as he saw it, to see their children "virtuously and religiously brought up to lead a godly and Christian life." This was for him the base of all education, its aim and its end: "En la sua voluntade e nostra pace – in His will is our peace." It is not surprising, therefore, that there was at Highbury during this period a great flowering of cultural and social activity – the Dramatic Society, the School Choir, in which he sang throughout as a member of the chorus, the School Camp which he never failed to visit.

In school and out, it was characteristic of him to permit his staff to do their job without interference; he trusted them and, as a result, they did not fail him, His life was bound up with the school and any contribution which any master or boy could and would make to the common life was gladly and gratefully accepted. To him the school was a family and it was with those who would not or could not realise this, that he found it hardest to be patient – "Ne Absiste" was the motto he chose for the school. Despite the disappointment and frustration of the War, despite ill-health and anxiety as to what the future had in store for the school, he has lived out this maxim in his own life to the full. We who remain will treasure his memory and remember with gratitude the service he both gave and won.

This article and the photograph (by Mr. L. Lincoln) appeared in *The Highburian Magazine*, Vol 1, No.2, of July 1953.

## Chapter Five
# *The new Headmaster*

When Highbury County reassembled on Monday 7 September 1953, there was a new Headmaster, Mr. R.J. King, M.A., who had previously been Acting Head of Holloway Secondary School. A staff meeting was called for the end of the afternoon, and later Ron Beverton described the proceedings at length in his diary:

> At the end of the afternoon was the staff meeting for which everyone had been waiting. The first of each year was of the greatest importance, but this one carried with it special interest. We were all anxious to see what new plans the new Headmaster had in store for us.
>
> The staff room was filled with the smoke-fog from nearly a score of pipes and cigarettes as the 'old hands' and the younger sat in their chairs round the walls waiting for the new Head to put in his appearance. He entered and there was a slight stir amongst the convocation. The air was alive with expectancy and I felt a wave of transitory sympathy for the man who had come into the room to face his 'staff' — there would be some who would accuse him, others who would ridicule and many who would criticise. Only a few would welcome him and the changes he brought with him.
>
> But Mr. King was tact itself. He began by thanking us and expressing his confidence in our co-operation. He admitted cautiously that he did not want to tread on anyone's toes and that for the present – at any rate – he was prepared to let most things go on as they had done before. First he wanted to see how the land lay and what was needed. There was an audible sigh of relief around the staff room. Then the business of the meeting was started. Small things first – that was how King wanted it – so we heard about boys who were absent and boys who wanted to leave, about school dates and school functions and the printing of a programme card containing the events of the forthcoming year. There was no opposition from anyone, only a slight difference of opinion between the Headmaster and Mr. Gage, the Games Master, over the facility of obtaining good dates for sports at Highams Park and the swimming gala. Hitherto the games department had been noted for its slowness in starting and now it seemed as though the new Head was going to make use of both the carrot and the whip to urge that department into a trot...! The engagement between the two protagonists had been interesting and foretold things to come. The Head said he thought there was no difficulty in arranging dates or acquiring the use of a Corporation

*The expanded staff in 1957 (as far as we can identify faces!):* <u>Back row</u>: *?, ?, G. Baker (Science), H.F. Caister (Geography), A. Baynham (French), ?, R. Dunkley (Geography),P. Nobes (English), G.W. Cobby (French) and D. Ward (English);*
<u>Centre row</u>: *?, B.K. Youngs (Biology), ?, Lee( Art & Drama), D. Lewis (Maths), G. Spurgeon (Games), D. Mallinson (Art), R. Liddamore (French), P. Clavey (Schoolkeeper), L.E. Lane (Craft) and J.M. Knowles (History etc);*
<u>Front row</u>: *Mrs.D. Gauld (Music), S.B. Davis (Chemistry), V.F. Gage (Games & PT), A.P. Chapman (Maths),S.E. Golding (Physics),R.J. King (Head), Mrs.P. Cobby (Secretary), L.H. Lincoln (Latin), C.J.K.Garrett (History), E.G. Taylor (R.I.) and E.S. Wood (English).*

swimming bath, and that if Gage thought he would meet with no luck, then perhaps he, King, could help him out. But Gage thought it advisable to wait another year before applying for dates in connection with the swimming gala.

But there were other things achieved, which was more than anyone could say of most of the previous staff meetings under the retiring Headmaster. Mr. King would look into the use of Highams Park for sports early in spring next year (instead of mid-summer as hitherto!) As regards staffing, he understood the difficulties involved and would indent as soon as possible for an extra man, preferably on the Geography staff as that seemed where the greatest deficiency lay. It looked as if Len Davies had been in early to see the 'new old man'. Sam Golding could expect to have a new Physics Lab as well: the old one was literally tumbling down about his ears!

That led on to the position of German and Latin in the school and a few words arose that made my blood boil secretly. Later on he, that is King, intended to make Latin more important in view of the needs of that language but he did not want to do it at the expense of German. Then he enquired of the staff generally how selection for either of these two languages went about. Mention was made of the boys choosing for themselves and of their parents' wishes having an influence in the matter … Then when I rose to point out that this was now no longer the case, Leech laughed and echoed that they were "only pulling your leg, Sir!" The laughter subsided and talk moved on to other less sensitive matters, but for some minutes I remained furious at what I considered a plot for the maintenance of the old system whereby the best boys went in for Latin and the mediocre came to me…

Heartened by the Headmaster's fresh progressiveness in matters pertaining to the school and still not a little sore over the German-Latin incident, I pressed for further changes in the school regulations. Mr. King had just expressed his keenness on Morning Assembly and intimated that he expected to see the staff attend as regularly as the boys. This would certainly mean a change of heart on the part of fifty per cent of the staff, myself included, so I thought the moment opportune for clearing up some of the rest of the ragged discipline in the school. I revised the question of boys appearing at Assembly still wearing their outdoor clothes, complete with caps, raincoats and satchels: Morning Assembly was hardly the place for that sort of haphazard turnout!

My suggestion met with sympathetic attention from Mr. King himself, who admitted how appalled he had been to see the school that very morning. The question of cloakrooms came into the argument and the new Headmaster saw that there was no valid reason for boys not getting rid of their raincoats and so on before coming into hall of a morning. That gave rise to attendance registers — quite another burning question. A few of us had been eager to see an "attendance period" with our forms in the morning, but so far nothing had come of the suggestion. Now, George Cobby, urged on by Dennis and a nudge from myself, got up to plead the cause.

This brought about quite a protracted debate on the subject. The question of times for Morning Assembly arose, of the times for bells, of the need for registration and a chance to "catch up on our forms" was bandied about. At the end of all this poor Mr. Howells, our Senior Master, made a rather unfortunate remark concerning the time of the first bell in the morning, giving the impression of complete unawareness of morning procedure. And he continued to stress his point fervently till the full realization of his blunder made him retire from the fray mortally wounded. But George's point won the day and he received the energetic support from all the younger members of the staff, together with the tacit sympathy from some of the elder. In future there would be five to ten minutes of a morning with forms then ten minutes for Assembly. It was by now beginning to look as if there were two forces lined up in the staff room. The younger generation was all out pressing for changes whilst the older generation with traditional reserve preferred to say little or offer only tentative objections in the hope of maintaining the *status quo*. By the time Colin came forward with his proposition for dividing the four Houses into a Senior and Junior — half the alignment was complete.

So the first staff Meeting under the new Headmaster came to a close. A new wind was blowing and clearing away the stale air of past years. There were changes in the offing and all the suggestions, apart from those of the Headmaster, had come from the younger section of the staff. Latent hopes for an improved system in Highbury County had now seen the light of day as had hopes for surviving. A final proposition, put forward by Dennis and eagerly backed by Leech, for greater responsibilities to be given to the prefects was also carried overwhelmingly. For in it we not only saw the general sloth of the prefectural hierarchy being shaken out of them, but an overall diminution of our own administrative tasks. For the first time both generations in the staff room were closely united: the prefects were to take over the active duty of patrolling the playgrounds and taking the lates! The staff were to remain nominally on duty, supervising the arrangements from the headquarters of the staff room.

The door of the staff room opened and the wind from the windows cleared the room of smoke. The sound of scraping chairs and the murmur of voices

*Mr. King and his wife at a Sixth Form dance, with Mike Edghill and Alice, who became his wife, and Bob Thomas and girlfriend (Photo: Mike Edghill)*

echoed in the corridor outside as we prepared to leave. The first day back at Highbury was over. Outside the autumn sunlight still shone through the leaves of the plane trees and the traffic still roared its way up the hill towards the Arsenal. I left the school building, said goodbye to my friends there and got on my cycle to begin the long ride home. I felt the ice had been broken and that it was good to be back at work once again.

## Dennis Ward

Another addition to the staff interested Ron Beverton – indeed the whole school – and that was Dennis Ward. Here is a comment Beverton made in his diary for September 1953, together with some remarks by David Perman.

 (RB)   Ward was stocky and dark. His body was broad and soft, his hair thick and wavy, his eyes protruding — in fact, he looked the perfect specimen of thyrotoxicosis. His voice came as a soft piping whisper. After a few days we learnt a little more about the newcomer. His career had not followed the usual routine of his colleagues. He had left school when he was sixteen. Now he was thirty-three. When he had left, school teaching had not even entered his thoughts. Instead he had taken an ordinary job, then served his six years in the Forces. On demobilisation he had entered Wadham College at Oxford aided by an Adult Education grant to study English – his subject today at Highbury. Up at Oxford he had won a blue for boxing and that had made quite a sensation in the otherwise somewhat conventional atmosphere of the staff-room.

(DP)  "Punchy" Ward (as we called him) was a refreshing addition to the English department and those of us taking English in the Sixth Form soon felt the benefit. He launched in at the first lesson by comparing the characterisation of the Prologue to Chaucer's *Canterbury Tales* with the novels of Raymond Chandler.

## The Rule of R.J. King

Mr. King's headship began rather differently from that of Mr. Marsh's "reign of terror" in 1928. As an egalitarian and devout Congregationalist, he was determined to rule by consensus, but with all the social and economic changes of the late 50s and early 60s he was not to have an easy time. In 1960, he told the audience at Speech Day in St. Pancras Town Hall that Italian-style shoes and clothes were having so great an influence among the boys that he had called a meeting of parents for a "frank discussion" of the problem. Another problem was the disquieting results in GCE Ordinary Level. He mentioned a meeting between three boys from the school and a girl from Highbury Hill – and she had nine GCE passes, more than all the boys together.

"The reason behind the failures and compromises is partly due to the fact that the boys are going through adolescence earlier nowadays. But their bodies grow more quickly than their minds. They are under constant pressure from the world outside school, and want independence, money and a higher standard of life at an earlier age. But I think the main cause is the lack of confidence among the boys – the lack of faith in their own abilities."

Mr. King returned to the topic in 1964, when he said: "I don't mind the clothes, the music, even the part-time work for wages of so many. What I deplore is their uniformity, their reluctance to stand up to the pressure of the mob." He said he had a sense of failure that 12 years before he had set out to help boys to realise themselves as individuals and he felt he had not succeeded. This theme of each boy being an individual had been in his mind the previous year, when he appealed to parents to help their sons to face problems with courage. There were small groups of boys, he said, who had been intolerant of individual boys who seemed to be "different". There was little, if any, sign of friction through colour, but boys had been subjected to mean and unworthy teasing for reasons of religion, or because they were not good at games, or were timid by nature.

Under his leadership, academic results improved and the Sixth Form continued to grow. Highbury boys were attending universities in many parts of the country. His greatest frustration was with the Victorian building. In 1958, he told the parents that the noise of lorries and buses in Highbury Grove not only affected work in the school, but sapped everyone's energy.

"I can only say that when five o'clock comes round I am dead whacked and tired. Sometimes, in my even moments, I wish we could have a fire!"

The problem of the premises was beginning to be solved in Mr. King's last years – but not in a way that he or the school expected or desired. That is a topic for the end of this book. For now, we can record the tribute paid by the Acting Head, Mr. Wood, at the 1965 Speech Day to Mr. King's 12 years as Headmaster of Highbury:

"No one who has attended a speech day during that time will have anything but admiration for the lucid, forthright and fascinating accounts of school activities that he reported year after year. They showed most vividly his enthusiasm for education, his concern for the boys he taught, his faith in the grammar school, and his essentially humane outlook, in which every boy in his charge was an individual to be guided and protected. We all owe him a debt for the example he gave of selfless absorption in all aspects of the school."

## Chapter Six
# *The Younger Generation*

As Ronald Beverton remarked in his diary, in 1953 the Highbury staff room was divided into two camps: "The younger generation was all out pressing for changes whilst the older generation with traditional reserve preferred to say little or offer only tentative objections in the hope of maintaining the *status quo*." Indeed, the younger generation soon began to socialise in a way that would have been unthinkable for the old hands.

There follow "appreciations" of three of the younger generation, together with the class lists that Colin Winter preserved over all these years!

## *GEORGE COBBY*

George himself provided these notes: "As I came from a similar background to that of my pupils, Highbury County was the ideal place to start my career in 1949. I was the luckiest member of staff in that I met my future wife there but, professionally, it taught me a great deal about the needs of both teaching and learning. So I became involved in examination reforms (a far cry from today's dumbing-down) and I realised that my future lay in training teachers, rather than in seeking promotion to what is now known as the Senior Management Team.

"To widen my experience I moved on from Highbury at the end of 1959. After seven years in a comprehensive (a risible term for what happened there!) I joined Borough Road College as a lecturer, eventually going to another outpost of London University's Institute of Education. There I achieved my ambitions with an ideal balance between administration and classroom. Then governments of both colours (but equally yellow) decided that we had too many teachers and I found myself redundant at the age of 54. After four years on the dole ("over-qualified") I was rescued by a couple of Buckinghamshire grammar schools where qualifications by experience were valued. I finished my career with an Indian summer back in the classroom, during which time I was Ofsted-ed – and passed.

"I enjoy pottering in the garden, history, photography, classical music and short touring holidays on the Continent."

## *PATRICIA COBBY*

Patricia Cobby (née Poulten), George's wife, will be remembered as the Highbury School Secretary from 1951-61. After raising a family, she took up

*George Cobby, Colin Winter and Dennis Lewis with Mr. R.J. King.*

charity work, first with the National Childbirth Trust. In four years, she trained from home 400 expectant mothers. This encouraged her to take up teaching, in which she graduated at the age of 44; she then spent 16 years inspiring youngsters in North and Northwest London, having the distinction of never having an examination failure. When she "retired" complementary medicine and animal welfare benefitted from her efforts. Patricia died in 1997.

## RONALD BEVERTON

Ronald J. Beverton came to Highbury County as German master in 1950, replacing Mr. Carmichael, who had taken up a teaching post in his native Scotland. Ronald was born in December 1923 at Ilford in Essex and attended Wanstead County High School, where he soon showed his talent for languages, particularly in German. Between 1936 and 1938 he took part in exchange visits to Leverkusen, near Cologne. There he made several friends in what was then National Socialist Germany, and had to cancel an intended visit to Germany in 1939 when war was declared. In October 1942 he was offered a place at Bristol University to read German & English.

As he said, he had "barely got his feet under the table" at University in the autumn of 1942, when he was conscripted for military service. At the suggestion of his German professor, he applied to join the Government Communications Bureau, which was part of MI6 – military counter espionage. What followed will be found in the Chapter, "The Cloak & Dagger War" elsewhere in this book. He was demobilised in 1947, married his wife Cynthia on 13th September that year and resumed his University studies at Bristol, where he gained his BA Honours degree in 1949.

Ronald took up his first teaching post at Highbury County School in September 1950, where he found himself joining a staff of much older masters many of whom had been at Highbury since the 1920s. He and the other "new boys" in the staff room soon formed a sort of "mutual support" group as they set about learning their trade.

After George and Patricia Cobby were married, they had set up home in an inexpensively rented flat in Stoke Newington, which although habitable, required a lot of cleaning and redecoration. Their new friends Cynthia and Ronald were established in their rented flat in Redbridge, East London, from where Ronald cycled to work at Highbury daily; at that time Ronald & Cynthia were keen cyclists. George recounts the amusing tale of a weekend dinner invitation, which he and Patricia had issued to the Bevertons. George and Patricia were busy sprucing up their flat for this engagement the following weekend, when there came a knock at the door. Opening the door in a somewhat dishevelled state revealed Ronald and Cynthia on the doorstep. George greeted them with embarrassment, pointing out that the invitation was for the following weekend, but they would be more than welcome to share a snack supper. "Thanks, but no," replied Ron, "we don't want to miss out on one of Pat's superb dinners." At this, Ronald apologised for the misunderstanding and he and Cynthia remounted their bicycles, and set off back to their home in East London. No offence was taken, and a great time was had by all the following Saturday.

One of Ron's former pupils remembers him as "fairly tall, with Nordic good looks, fair-haired, with piercing blue eyes and a sharp aquiline nose and high cheek-boned features. He had a presence in front of a class, which immediately let us know that this was not a teacher we could play up. In fact he never found it necessary to raise his voice, or to resort to throwing chalk or blackboard dusters to maintain discipline, as did some of the other masters. Like most of the teachers, he wore an academic gown, but seemed not to need to carry a sawn-off billiard cue or blackboard pointer, as some of the older generation of teachers did, by way of an implied threat to trouble makers.

"He certainly knew his subject, and had the knack of teaching the complexities of German grammar, in an understandable way. He also possessed a patience with lads who like me, continued to have difficulty with the finer points even into the Sixth form, and I owe my fluency in the language even now to his perseverance. By comparison with the older masters on the staff, he also had a human side, when it was appropriate for him to relax discipline with the Sixth form, and when he became involved with producing the school plays. He and his wife also supported the school's social activities, when it came as a huge surprise to some of us hormonal young lads, that some of our masters actually had attractive & shapely young wives. We remember today many of the masters for their foibles and irascibility. Ron Beverton is one of the few we remember as a really great teacher, a decent sportsman and all round *nice bloke*."

Ronald and Cynthia had three children, Elizabeth, born in 1954, son Martin born in 1955, now a doctor, and Julie, born in 1957, now a nursing sister at a hospital in Essex. Ronald left Highbury County in 1958 to take up a new post at Harold Hill Grammar School, where he taught until moving again to teach at Harlow, and finally to Nicholas School in Harlow before his retirement in 1989. Sadly Ronald Beverton died, aged 77 in January 2000.

*[We are extremely grateful to Cynthia Beverton for allowing us unprecedented access to Ronald's personal diaries, giving us a unique insight into the contemporary staff room. Thanks to her also for the loan of hitherto classified tapes recalling his wartime activities as a counter-espionage agent for MI6.]*

*"The Highbury Gang" reunion in March 1993 – back: Brian Youngs, George Cobby and Ron Beverton; seated: Dennis Lewis, Pat Cobby and Colin Winter.*

# COLIN WINTER

Colin ('Wally') Winter is a Kentish man, who came to Highbury County as third Maths teacher under Mr. A. Chapman in 1949. A keen sportsman, not only did he take an active part in supervising school games afternoons at Highams Park and cross-country running at Parliament Hill Fields, but also wielded a formidable bat in the Staff vs. Boys matches. On at least one occasion he ran most of the cross-country course backwards, keeping an eye on the stragglers to make sure none of us took the short cut to the finish. He was firm with his classes, but generally respected by the boys.

He joined Mr. Beverton in leading the first School holiday trip abroad to Germany in 1954, and supported the school social activities such as the monthly dances and theatre trips *inter alia.* He sang with the school choir with a rich baritone voice, was an enthusiastic rower, and many at Highbury will remember that his soccer refereeing was the cause of some derision! Colin claims that his own mathematics education was 'prehistoric,' so he became involved in "bringing school work into the twentieth century".

In 1955 Colin Winter left Highbury to take up a post at Colfe's School in South London. When Colin was invited to attend an evening function prior to joining his new school, he apologised for his absence by informing them that it was the day of the Highbury County School Regatta and Summer Ball. He later taught at Brunel University, tempting mathematicians into teaching.

Today Colin lives with his second wife in Alderley Edge, Cheshire, and has children and grandchildren scattered around the world. He leads an active retirement, does a fair amount of holiday travelling, and is involved in a choral society, classes and clubs, which keep him quite busy.

Colin still has fond memories of Highbury County, where, as he says:

"Those years are very bright to me. We were all at the beginning of our careers, with a big age gap between the senior staff and us, so we were the reformers and shakers. We regard it as a happy time. Highbury was a very effervescent place, where absolutely everything - triumphs and disasters – happened, but we felt that we moved the place on a bit."

## Colin Winter's Class Lists 1949 - 54

Colin was kind enough to provide the following Register lists of classes he taught. He apologises for any errors, for which he blames his inability to read his own writing after so many years.

54

## 1949 – 50

**Form 2G:** Ambler, Gordon; Ansell, Ian; Batchelor, Raymond; Bevan; Biggs, Leonard; Boyle, Brian; Bright; Burwash; Carney, David; Coombes, John; Cohen, Michael; Craven; Dent, Robert; Downing, Victor; Farley; Glasberg, Joseph; Greenfield, Alan; Harding; Hiam, Edward; Hunt; Hurley, Derek; Johnson, Thomas; Jones Geoffrey; Lambert, John; Lowe, Peter; Parnall, Alan; Pepper; Pingree, John; Pitt, John; Plummer; Rosefield, A; Samuels; Savin, Peter; Seymour; Short; Simpson; Smith, Roy; Southwell, Leonard; Stagg, Michael; Strutton; Webster; Wilson, John; Wood.

*(Colin Winter notes that there seem to have been 44 pupils numbered in this class, but doubts that overcrowding was ever so bad, and suggests that there must have been some reshuffling. As this was the year of my own intake, I can confirm that according to my memory, Burwash, Carney, Glasberg, Harding, Lowe, Pingree, Southwell and Strutton were reshuffled, mostly into the 'A' (Latin) stream, while Derek Hurley dropped out through truanting until finally expelled. —Brian Boyle).*

**Form 3A:** Beaumont, Bickerton, Collins, B., Dawson, Edwards, G., Edwards, J., Finley, Gray, Hamilton, Herbert, Jay Jenkins, King, Lewins, McInnes, Martin, Mills, Moore, Morris, Parsons, Pendrill, Pitfield, Pollard, Reddy, F., Rolfe, Saunders, Searl, Shanes, Spiegelstein, Tennant, Thomas, A., Webb, Wright, A. & Wright, M.

**Form 3B:** Bloxham, Breckman, M., Bryden, Calcutt, Coldwell, Coleman, Colley, Coombes, J., Corton, Day, Dyer, J., Farrell, Gordon, Hayden, Herbert, Hex, W., Hunt, JE, Hunt, JL, Kimpton, Lasky, Leeson, Leigh, McHardy, Marcovich, Offwood, Page, Phair, Plummer, N., Radlett, Robinson, G., Simper, Sowden, Taylor, Tye, Ubly, Venitt, S.

**Form 4C:** Abrahams, Black, Clarke, Compton, Cook, Dobson, Flack, Goulding, Harris, Harman, Kinton, Keightley, Kent, Little, Mowatt, Mutler, Oldham, Pepper, Reid, T., Rose, Salmon, Sloan, Smith, Soper, Stacey, Staples, Tasker, Williams, Wilson, R., Young.

**Remove Form B:** Baker, Barnes, Blake, Cable, Chidley, Chipperfield, Ford, Fudge, Goode, Gray, D., Gray, R., Greenwood Harman, Harold, Holmes, McCarthy, McMillan, Manning, May, Middleton, Moore, Mulholland, Prytherch, Saachs, Sassoon, Snook, Steggles, Stephenson, Symons, Thoroughgood, Tomkins, Whitehead, Winslett.

**Form 5A:** Ansell, Barrett, Bennett, Black, Brittain, Butler, Caiger, Carlton, Chapman, Curtis, Felstead, Fox, Gibson, Groves, Hadley, Harman, Irving, Lack, McKenzie, Moreign, Portch, Pudner, Quattromini, Rabbinovitz, Reynolds, Sealy, Shipperlee, Studling, Trollope, Trompetto, Wilkinson, Williams, Wright.

**Form 2H:** Roberts, Rockingham, G; Robinson, G; Rowe, Sandell, A; Sann, Saunders, Short, D; Short, G.; Simpkins, A.; Skipp, Smith, G.; Smith, R; Smith, T; Stanger, Steinhart, Syer, Taylor, Thomas, A; Thynne, Twohey, Twynham, Tyler, Venitt, S; Watson, A; Webb, Wetherall, White, J; White, V; Wilkinson, Williams, Woodward, Woods, Woolf & Zusman.

**Form 3B:** Allen, Bevan, Chamberlain, Clarke, Cook, Corp, R.; Coulson, Day Fogg, Hammond, Harding, Harrison, Howlett, Jelliman, Kelly, Lavine, Millichamp, Mitchell, Nye, Pepper, Platzer, Plummer, N.; Preston, Robens, Sanderson, J.; Short, H.; Smith, B.; Smith, W.; Spendiff, Tatum, Thwaites, Vargo & Ward, B.

**Form 3N:** Ambler, Gordon; Ansell, Ian; Batchelor, Raymond; Bevan,?; Biggs, Leonard; Boyle, Brian; Brown,?; Clarke, ?; Cohen, Michael; Dent, Robert; Downing, Victor; Edghill, Michael; Grablof, Jack; Greenfield, Alan; Hiam, Edward; Hunt, M; Jennings, William; Johnson, Thomas; Jones, Geoffrey; Jones, Reginald; Lambert, John; Moore, Kenneth; Parnall, Alan; Pingree, John; Pitt, John; Rosefield, M; Savin, Peter; Seymour,?; Short.?; Smith, Roy; Stagg, Michael; Webster,?; Wilson, John & Wood,?

**Form 4S:** Beaumont, Bickerton, Collins, Copeland, Dawson, Edwards, G., Edwards, J., Finlay, Gray, Hamilton, Hart, Herbert, Jay, Jenkins, King, Lewins, McInnes, Martin, Miller, Moore, Morris Parsons, Pendrill, Pitfield, Reddy, Reddy, F.; Rolfe, Saunders, Searl, Shanes, Spiegelstein, Tennant, Thomas, R., Webb, Wright, A.; Wright, M.

**Remove Form O:** Baker, Barker, Bird, Bowman, Bowring, Brice, Brown, Cronin, Culmer, Davis, Evans Garner, Hagerman, Hart, Jose, Lucas, Mason, Meechum, Peretz, Phillips, Read, Ruggles, Shirley, Simper, Smith, Startup, Upcroft, Wiener, Wilmot.

**Form 5M:** Baker, Barnes, Blake, Cable, Chidley, Chipperfield, Ford, Fudge, Goode, Gray, D.W., Greenwood, Harman, May, Middleton, Moore, Mulholland, Sassoon, Snook, Steggles, Stephenson, Symonds, Thurogood, Tompkins, Triefeldt, Neufeld, Streamer, Townley, Woolf, and Smith.

**Form 2H:** Adams, Ambridge, Armsby, Barber, Bardsley, Barrs, Broughton, Bruce, Butt, Carey, Chandler, Carne, Clark, B., Clark, R., Collins, Conway, Coote Cornhill, Corp, Cram, Crawford, Davis, I, Davis, S.G., Dix, Doward, Downes, Eaton, Elly,  Fantom, Field, E., Field, J., Finnion, Fitzgibbon, Vrahimedes.

**Form 3B:** Allen, Andrews, Atkinson, Baker, Bennett, Barrett,C; Barrett, D; Bartram, Bedford, Beesley, Blitstein, Bloxham, Blyth, Bolden, Bolton, Bourne,

Briers, Burt, Caffel, Caskie, Clarke,P; Clements, Cohen, Coleclough, Cook, Cork Cranham, Davies, Dickens, Dobson, Embleton, Everett, Felton, Fenn, Fields, Ford, Hodge.

**Form 4R**: Ambler, Gordon; Ansell, Ian; Batchelor, Raymond; Bevan, Biggs, Leonard; Boyle, Brian; Brown, Cohen, Michael; Dent, Robert; Downing, Victor; Edghill, Michael; Grablof, Jack; Greenfield, Alan; Hiam, Edward; Hunt, Jennings, William; Johnson, Thomas; Jones, Geoffrey; Jones, Reginald; Lambert, John; Moore, Kenneth; Parnall, Alan; Pingree, John; Pitt, John; Rosefield, A; Savin, Peter; Seymour, Smith, Roy; Stagg, Michael; Wilson, John; Wood.

**Remove Form A:** Beaumont, Bickerton, Collins, Copeland Dawson, Edwards, G; Edwards, J; Finley, Grey, Hamilton, Herbert, Jay, Jenkins, King, Lewins, McInnes, Martin, Mills, Moore, Oughten, R.; Parsons, Pendrill, Pittfield, Pollard, Reddy, F; Saunders, Searl, J; Shanes, Spiegelstein, Tennant, Thomas, R.; Webb, Wright, A.; Wright, M.

**Form 5M:** Barker, Bird, Bowman, Bowring, Brice, Brown, Cronin, Davis, Garner, Hagerman, Hart, Lucas, Meechum, Peretz, Phillips, Read, Ruggles, Shirley, Simper, Smith, Startup, Upcroft, Weiner, Willmot, Woodward, Wray.

## 1952-53

**Form 3F:** Adams, Ambridge, Butt, Carne, Collins, Corpe, R.; Davidson, Davies, Doward, Downes, Eaton, Field, J.; Fitzgibbon, Foster, Gibbs, Gregory, Harkman, Hibberd, Huxham, Ings, Inman, Morecroft, Munci, Oliver, Quatrominni, Richardson, Thomas, A.; Thorncroft, Thorpe, Tynan, Vrahimedes, Warren, Wood, Woodford, Woodrow.

**Form4/3:** Barker, Barrett, C.; Corpe, R.; Cranham, Dickens, Everett, Felton, D.; Fenn, Ford, Godfrey, Hodson, James, Kendall, Kipps, Lark, S.; Leibovitch, Merino, McKay, Pearce, Portz, Robinson, G.; Rowe, Saunders, Seddon, Short, Simpkins, A.; Steinhart, Thomas, T.; Twynham, West, Williams, White, V.

**Remove Form 2:** Allen, Ansell,I.; Austin, Bevan, H.; Bevan, R.; Biggs, L.; Bright, Bucks, Chamberlain, Cook, Corpe, R.; Davies, G.; Davis, D.; Dent, R.; Edghill, M.; Grablof, J.; Greenfield, A.; Harrison, Jennings, W.; Johnson, T.; Lavine, Lowe, P.; Michell, New, Parnall, A.; Pingree, J.; Platzer, Roberts, Simpson, Stagnell, R.; Strutton, Tatum, Ward, B.; Wilson, J.

**Fifth Form 1:** Breckman, M.; Davies, Gordon, Hayden, Jay, Lancaster, Lee, Leeson, Lewins, Mills, Morris, Offwood, Oughton, R.; Parsons, Perlmutter, Pitfield, Radlett, Rolfe, Searl, J.; Spiller, Swindon, Tennant, Thomas, R.; Webb, Wright, A.; Wright, M.

**Sixth Form:** Ambrose, J.; Blumenthal, P.; Dixon, Harman, Harrison, Ingless, R.; Morrison, Peretz, Weiner, P.

## 1953 – 54

**Form 3B** – Class photograph *(courtesy Eddie Moss)*

Allen, Bainbridge, Bell, Clark, Cross, Day, Edwards, Evans, Foster, B. Foster, J.; Freeman, Gorton, Green, Griffiths, Horn, Hurd, Jackson, Jones, Lane, Loflins, Mann, McKeon, Miles, Moss, E.; Musgrave, Newland, Norris, Owen, Pamment, Pash, Pudner, Ranger, Rawlins, Saxby, Smith, Tupper, Turner, Wheeler, Wills.

**Form 4S:** Adams, Ambridge, Carne, Collins, Corpe, R.; Davidson, Davies, Doward, Downes, Easton, Field, J.; Fitzgibbon, Gibbs, Gregory, Harkman, Hibberd, Huxham, Inman, Morecroft, Muncey, Oliver, Pain, Parikh, S.; Quatrominni, Richardson, Thorncroft, Thorpe, Tynen, Vrahimedes, Warren, Wood, Woodford.

**Remove Form O:** Andrews, Atkinson, Barrett, C.; Barham, Blitstein, Bolton, Bloxham, Caffel, Clarke, Corpe, R.; Felton, D.; Haydock, Holden, Hornett, Ingless, R.; Kipps, Lafar, Lark, Lock, Lovegrove, Miller, Myers, Pears, Polly, Saunders, Rowe, Roberts, Simpkins, A.; Squires, Taylor, Twohey, Twynham, Tyler, White, Wilkinson, Woodward.

**Form 5M:** Ambler, G.; Ansell, I.; Bevan, Biggs, L.; Boyle, B.; Brown, Dent, R.; Downing, V.; Edghill, M.; Grablof, J.; Greenfield, A.; Hunt, Jennings, W.; Johnson, T.; Jones, G.; Jones, R. Lambert, J.; Moore, K.; Parnall, A.; Pingree, J.; Rosefield, Savin, P.; Smith, R.; Wilson, J.

**Form 5T:** Brown, Davies, Fogg, Hex, J.; Lavine, Ward.

**Sixth Form:** Blumenthal, P.; Dixon, K.; Harman, Harrison, Peretz, Triefeldt, J. Weiner, P.;

## Chapter Seven
# *Confessions of the Beaks*

The following questions, apart from the last two, are the same as those first posed in 1950s editions of *The Highburian Magazine*. In the July 1953 edition, the respondents were Physics master, Sam Golding, who is sadly no longer with us, and Biology master, Brian "Bunny" Youngs. We regret that Art master W.H. Laurie and Mr. "Nobby" Knowles are no longer available to resit the interrogation to which they submitted for the December edition of the *Highburian*; French master George Cobby and English master E.S. Wood were interrogated for the July, 1957 edition. We are grateful to Messrs. Cobby (GWC) and Youngs (BKY) for agreeing to update their responses half a century later.

*Q:     Why did you become a teacher?*

GWC: I won a free place at a grammar school in 1938, when even state grammar schools were fee-paying. Everyone has the right to – and should have the opportunity of – a good education and, then aged 21, I wanted to be part of providing this opportunity.

BKY:  My father was a headmaster, and it was always assumed that I too would teach.

*Q:     Can you enjoy life on a teacher's pension?*

GWC: Yes, but only because I've spent a lifetime having to live on a teacher's salary!

BKY:  This does not really apply in my case. Having resigned – or should I say RETIRED? – from teaching in 1959, I entered practice (as an osteopath). I withdrew my superannuation – approximately £450 and bought a second-hand Armstrong-Siddeley Sapphire. It was a wonderful car. (Armstrong-Siddeley produced a range of luxury cars, of which the Sapphire was the height of luxury at the time.)

*Q:     What is your favourite pastime?*

GWC: I see that in 1957 I replied: "swimming." But I wish I really could swim. My "dropped foot" has always been a hindrance. Nowadays I very much enjoy music, history and travel, but especially the company of family and friends.

BKY:  No one overall, but enjoying married and family life comes high on my list. I also enjoy reading, squash, travel, and trekking.

*Q:     What is your favourite book or TV Soap?*

GWC: *Cyrano de Bergerac*, which I gave as my favourite book in 1957, is of course actually a play. We were then studying it in the Sixth Form and I found it profoundly moving. My answer today would probably be : "Whatever history book I am currently reading." In those olden days the *Goon Show* spawned much high quality humour. Unfortunately much of today's TV humour is "presented" by foul-mouthed, flatulent, semi-literate professional epileptics! Having been born in the East End, I find *EastEnders* along with its provincial cousins, unwatchable. *M*A*S*H* was the greatest TV to come out of the USA: Groucho Marx with compassion. My old colleagues will tell you that I haven't changed since the Fifties. Untrue! I am now much more diplomatic!

BKY:  That's difficult! At University my favourite book was Aldous Huxley's *Point and Counterpoint* and there were many others. Nowadays I read books all the time, and usually have about six on the go. Favourite TV programmes include *Frazier, Coupling, M*A*S*H, Cheers* and *Dad's Army.*

*Q:     What is your opinion of Modern Art?*

GWC: Largely unprintable! The most decent thing in the Tate Modern is Rodin's "The Kiss," I think it is wonderful.

BKY:  I'm generally unimpressed.

*Q:     What is your favourite film?*

GWC: My favourite film stars are those who populated the most sophisticated comedies of the Thirties and Forties. They had so much more subtlety and poise than today's bimbos and hunks.

BKY: *La Ronde de l'Amour* with Anton Wallbrook.

*Q:     What was the most embarrassing moment of your career?*

GWC: I don't want to remember it!

BKY:  I would have liked being caught in *flagrante delicto* with Brigitte Bardot, but had no such luck!

*Q:     What is your most abiding memory of Highbury?*

GWC: It changed my life.

BKY:  There are so many. Scoring a perfect square-cut for 4 in the Boys v. Staff match, and then being out for 5!

*Q:     Any other comment you would care to add?*

GWC: In 1957 we were asked which law we would most like to break, if we were given impunity. My answer was, at the time: The law on Income Tax.

The whole system of taxation remains unfair and obscure. Successive Chancellors have not dared tell the Truth, for fear of committing political suicide. What the Hell do they do with our money, anyway?

BKY: I had nine years at Highbury, and enjoyed every minute, thanks to the boys – great lads. We had a great Head in "Boggy" Marsh, and the staff and the atmosphere of the staff-room were great also. R.J. King was also a fine Head. Other characters I remember fondly were the Schoolkeeper, Percy Clavey, and School Secretary, the late Pat Cobby, who was a lovely lady and made excellent coffee!

Pat, who met her husband, George while working at the School, sadly died about ten years ago.

Brian Youngs celebrated his 80th birthday in February 2004. When we contacted him for this feature, he told us that he and his wife Anne took their holiday in September last, trekking in the High Atlas Mountains in Morocco. During a subsequent skiing trip, Anne suffered a fall, in which she broke her pelvis. Anne recovered from that accident but it reactivated her cancer and sadly she died in May 2004.

*Brian Youngs (right) reluctantly posing with Dennis Ward and Bill Laurie in Highbury Fields, while the three were on duty as the "Purity Patrol" to stop boys consorting with the girls from Highbury Hill.*

# Chapter Eight
# *Highbury under Canvas*

For many boys, summer camps were the most memorable part of their Highbury school years. In an age when few working class families had holidays of more than the occasional day trip (apart from hop-picking, which was more popular in east and south London), school camps played an important role in the community: they took children off the dusty streets and put them in healthy rural surroundings where they had to learn "to pull their weight" and be members of a team. They fulfilled a similar function to the camps run by the Boy Scouts and Boys' Brigade. The Highbury camps were begun by E.G. Taylor in 1931, with the first camp at Seaton on the coast of East Devon. He was certainly aware of the social role that camp played: at the time E.G. was also a part-time curate in Hackney as well as a teacher. The Seaton camps continued until Highbury County closed in the 1960s, apart from the war years when agricultural camps were held instead.

## My Memories of Winsford Camp, Somerset :1945-1949
## By T.G. Duthie

I am uncertain as to when the concept of Agricultural Camps was first introduced, but I can only assume that the idea was a product of the Second World War and was a way of helping with the war effort in general. I do not know for certain, but I would imagine that the camps first came into being during the early years of the War, i.e. 1940-41 and were organised by the Ministry of Agriculture, Fisheries & Food as far as the provision of camping gear, tents, marquees, cooking utensils and kitchen ranges were concerned.

My first experience of Winsford Camp was during the summer holidays of 1945, my first summer at Highbury County. Going from memory, about 70 boys under the supervision of our divinity teacher, the Revd. E.G. Taylor and a couple of other teachers attended the camp. Revd. Taylor was known by all the boys simply as E.G. and we addressed him as such on all occasions. He was in effect treated as a father figure and was held in high regard by both the boys and fellow teachers. Strict discipline was maintained and high standards of personal hygiene and general cleanliness were imposed throughout the camp. The boys were hired out to local farmers mainly to weed crops and to carry out work in the company of permanent farm labourers. As far as the wage rates were concerned, payment for the labour carried out, which on certain farms was quite arduous, was abysmal. On a personal basis I was paid at the rate of an old sixpence an hour when I first started work on a farm in the summer of 1946. At my first camp in 1945, I was considered by E.G. to be too small to be able to work on a farm (I was nearly 12) and was, therefore, employed in the Cooks' Tent for that year. Being in the Cooks' Tent entitled you to no pay but covered your food! Once we were able to start working on farms, some of the boys had the opportunity of meeting former prisoners-of-war who quite frequently married local girls and remained in Britain working on farms after hostilities had ended. In addition to the camp at Winsford, there were two other camps both situated in Somerset, at Wiveliscombe and Williton. I did not know anybody who attended these camps so I am not able to give you any insight into the running of these camps, but presumably they were run on the same lines as Winsford.

One of my earliest memories is the V.J. (Victory over Japan) celebrations which took place in August 1945 in one of the fields on the farm where our camp was pitched. Wood was gathered from the forest adjoining our camp over many days and the fire was burning for over 24 hours – great excitement for a boy just coming up to 12 years of age!

We worked on average from about 8/8.30 in the morning until about 5/5.30 in the evening. If we were fortunate we would be collected by the farmer who was employing us and returned to the camp in the evening in the farmer's transport. Quite often, however, we had to make our own way by bicycle to the farm in question, sometimes involving a round journey of up to 8/9 miles per day. I cannot now remember whether we were paid for travelling time or not.

My one abiding memory of camp life/farm life was the never ending feeling of hunger. We were given three slices of bread with various fillings which was expected to keep us going until dinner in the evening. Invariably the sandwiches were devoured by midday after which we had to forage from the land, preferably carrots or kale or from the permanent labourers. I cannot recall a single instance where the farmer's wife ever provided me with any food or drink so you can imagine how ravenous we were by the time we arrived back at camp in the evening. The only exception to this was when we were employed in the harvesting of the corn and, by tradition, farmers were expected to provide rough cider and scones and cream in view of the fact that all the boys and permanent labourers would be expected to carry on working until between 8 and 9 at night. On some farms, I seem to remember, you were required to work on a Saturday morning until midday but on most farms it was a 5 day week as far as the boys were concerned.

Saturday afternoons were spent clearing up the camp site in preparation for the weekly inspection by E.G. on Sunday morning. As an incentive to the winning tent, a privilege was granted to every member of that tent which

*Boys at Winsford Camp in the 1940s.*

invariably involved extra food. Sunday lunch, which was personally cooked and supervised by E.G., was by far the best meal of the week and afterwards most of us spent the afternoon either asleep or resting before having tea and going to church in Winsford in the evening. This pattern of life was followed for the whole of our time at camp. The only break was the one day we used to visit Minehead which was about nine miles away from camp on the coast. As far as I can remember, even just after the war there was a Butlins Holiday Camp in existence there.

After such a long lapse of time, it is strange what things still linger in the mind. One of the most vivid of my memories is the recollection of receiving at the end of my last camp in 1949 the sum of three crisp new blue £1 notes which represented my total earnings for the whole of the six weeks and that included a unique bonus of £1 paid to me by the farmer for whom I had worked for the whole of that summer. As far as I know that was the one and only record of a bonus being paid to anyone throughout the history of Winsford Camp.

The last agricultural working camp was in 1949 and I left Highbury after returning from camp in early September to start my working career. I would have dearly wished to have carried on into the Sixth Form and ultimately to university. However, in those far off days a working class boy's normal expectation was to leave at 16 with the equivalent of the present day GCSE or 'O' Levels. Then it was called General School Certificate with exemption from matriculation. In my year of approximately 95 boys for example, only one boy (who was best man at my wedding) went on to get his degree at Cambridge. As regards the Sixth Form, I believe only 10-15 boys from the whole year went on to study until they were 18. These figures give you some idea of how much opportunities have improved for the working class boy. I read recently that approximately 40% of students progress on to a university education. Good luck to them – I certainly envy them.

Although I did not fully realise it at the time, I consider I was privileged to have been educated at Highbury County and, in spite of all the hardships at Winsford Camp, I don't think I would have changed anything at all.

## Memories of Williton and Seaton
## By David Perman

Tom Duthie is correct: Williton Agricultural Camp was run on similar lines to that at Winsford. I went there in my first summer at Highbury, 1948, when I too was considered too young for field work and put in the cookhouse. The camp was run by Stan Wood and Lindsey Lane, who came accompanied by wives and daughters – a distinguishing mark from the camps of the celibate E.G. Taylor which I later attended at Seaton. The Wood daughters were roughly the same age as me but shyness and cookhouse duties kept us apart.

Williton is a hamlet a few miles inland from the village of Watchet, which itself is not far from Minehead on the Somerset coast. The camp consisted of a collection of bell tents and two large, brown marquees – one as the headquarters tent and the other as cookhouse and dining room – all pitched on a meadow sloping gently down to a pond, on the opposite side of which stood a large farmhouse. There were three or four of us smaller boys, or "sproggs", who did not work in the fields, including Roy Ingless. Our duties were to keep the camp site scrupulously tidy and to assist Mr. and Mrs. Wood in preparing the evening meal: peeling potatoes occupied much of our day. Our mornings began with clearing up after breakfast – we were spared its preparation, this being a job for older boys – then we had to roll up the sides of the marquee so that a good draught of air blew through. We had the same sandwich lunch as boys out on the farms, but the bonus of being able to rest in our tents for the early part of the afternoon. I sometimes forewent that pleasure and explored the bracken slopes of the nearby Quantocks. My best memories of Williton are of sing-songs around a camp fire and watching the final part of a wheat harvest being cut, with old boys stacking the stooks while the farmer stood with his gun waiting for the rabbits to flee their ever decreasing hide-out.

After a year's gap, I went in the summer of 1950 to the first of E.G. Taylor's postwar camps at Seaton. It had a more relaxed atmosphere than agricultural camp at Williton. On the other hand, we still had kit inspections and there were bugle calls for Reveille, Cookhouse, Last Post, etc. As there was no farm work to be done, there was a greater emphasis on sports and outings. To the west of Seaton was the tiny village of Beer where some of the older boys went for what else but ... In the other direction, there was the five-mile landslip leading on to Lyme Regis and made famous in *The French Lieutenant's Woman*.

We also sang in the church choir at Seaton. I went to E.G.'s camp three years running, finishing up as "Quartermaster". Both camps were well-run and full of good fun and comradeship.

*The Highburian Magazine* reported in July 1957 that "the School Camp began on 26 July 1956, when about 70 boys assembled at Waterloo Station for the annual pilgrimage. Some were new boys to the camp, while others had up to five years' experience. Even the Old Boys were unable to shake off the Camp. Some of them remembered their leaders of a few years

*Summer camp at Williton in 1948, with the families of Messrs. Wood and Lane. Below: kit inspection for the cookhouse tent; left to right: Porch, Ian Kay, Derek Gray, Perman and Ingless.*

back, and returned as officers. Mr. Golding brought experience, and Mr. Spurgeon vigour to the proceedings, which remained under Mr. Taylor's benign control. The Camp was held at Colyford, two miles from Seaton, in a new field larger than the old site, and on a gently sloping hillside. The weather was hot for the first few days, but on the Saturday night a storm blew in from the sea and the large marquee collapsed. On a later occasion during a storm, the older boys took down this same tent in the middle of the night, to prevent it from tearing. The weather of 1956 is notorious, and Seaton did not escape the widespread rain; the trips to smugglers' caves and mackerel fishing, having to be constantly cancelled. It did not rain every day however; three were extraordinarily warm, and the remainder were cool but dry."

## Chapter Nine
# *School Journeys*

It is sometimes assumed, when Old Highburians sit around reminiscing, that the first organised trip abroad after the war was that to Germany at the instigation of Messrs. Beverton and Winter. Important as that trip was, it was not the first (*writes David Perman*). In the spring of 1951 a party from the Fifth Form was taken to Belgium by the art master, Bill Laurie. We travelled by train to Dover, thence by ferry to Ostend, and then train to Bruges which became our headquarters for a week's stay. We stayed in the small but comfortable Hotel Venise du Nord (*see picture below*) named as such because Bruges, with its canals, is often called the "Venice of the North".

The purpose of the trip was decidedly cultural. We visited all the galleries and important churches of Bruges and Ghent, learned the intricacies of Flemish painting – for example how to tell a Hubert Van Eyck from a Jan Van Eyck and both from an Anthony Van Dyck – maybe spent much too long examining Gerard David's *Judgement of Cambyses* in which a corrupt judge is skinned alive, saw how the widows made lace in the Béguinage, went on a canal boat (of course) and even visited Brussels in that primitive era before it acquired either the European Common Market or a metro system. And Bill Laurie was a well-informed guide – it takes skill to sell the beauties of Belgium!

*The trip to Bruges with Bill Laurie (left) – photo thanks to Terry Woodford.*

# Holidays in Germany

Low cost holidays abroad were proposed for the school in the July 1953 edition of *The Highburian Magazine* as a joint venture by German master, the late Ron Beverton and Maths master Colin Winter (*writes Brian Boyle*).

There were two alternative proposals. The first would be an exchange visit with a school near Cologne. This would involve travelling in a party to Leverkusen, where accommodation would be arranged in the homes of boys at school there. In return their families would entertain a German boy for a similar period in England. This proposal seems not to have found support in the school, for it never happened. The second proposal was to be limited to fifteen boys, who would travel by boat and train to Cologne and spend the first fortnight of the summer holidays walking through the hills along the Rhine to Mainz. Accommodation would be in excellent German Youth Hostels; a really good way to see one of the most interesting areas in Germany. Preference would be given to Sixth formers and German sets in the fifth and Remove forms. The latter proposition was successful, for in *The Highburian* for July 1955 an anonymous correspondent penned an account, of which the following is an edited version.

Undeterred by the description of this as a walking holiday, twenty boys turned up at Victoria Station on 22 July for the night boat train to Ostend. Excitement kept most of them awake during the crossing, so that next day only a few felt inclined to tackle the long climb to the top of the Cathedral for their first real look at Germany.

The holiday really began for most of them when, after the discomforts of the train ride, they emerged into the peace and sunshine of the Mosel Valley. Here they bathed in the river and climbed through the vineyards up the steep sides of the valley to the skyline. They now sustained their only casualty when "Slash," while glissading down from the heights, failed to notice his companions make a sharp right turn, and projected himself on to the roadway ten feet below! They wandered down the Mosel from Trier to Brodenbach, enjoying sunshine most of the time, and passing pleasant hours in riverside cafes in the evenings.

Then a fairly stiff walk over the hills took them to the "Pearl of the Rhine" at Boppard. Despite their fatigue, at the Youth Hostel that evening they challenged a party of German girls to a curious game of handball, the rules of which seemed to alter largely to their disadvantage, as the game progressed. However the effect was to ease, rather than create any international tensions!

The Rhine valley is wider and less intimate than the Mosel, and there is a bustle of road, rail and river traffic along the length of the gorge. So they left the valley, and walked along tracks through isolated villages on either side, where their arrival created something of a local event and their reception was always friendly.

The Hotel at Bacharach is a very fine medieval castle, towering above the town. Their enthusiasm for it diminished somewhat when they discovered that the Warden had confused their booking date, and they had to sleep in the dungeons! At Assmanshausen they shortened their walk by taking a ride on the "Sesselbahn" or chair lift, dangling their legs a hundred feet above the treetops. A little further on they horrified the local photographer by choosing to be photographed against the impressive background of the entrance to the Rhine Gorge, instead of against the enormous and ugly (*sic*) statue of "Germania" as most visitors were.

Most of the return journey to Cologne was achieved by steamer on the Rhine, with interruptions to stretch their legs at Koblenz, Bad Honnef and Bonn. Bad Honnef was chiefly remembered for magnificent ice creams served at a restaurant at the top of the Drachenfels, commanding a view of around fifty miles.

One of the features of the trip was the daily issue of money for midday meals, which the boys spent in restaurants or on packed lunches. This provided them with good practice for their German in the shops, and some surprises for their digestions. In retrospect the rain showers and foot blisters were less remembered than the friendship and laughter, it was hoped that this first experience of Youth Hostelling abroad might inspire some to undertake further such tramping holidays in future years.

Stan Venitt was a regular contributor to *The Highburian*, and from the same issue comes the following light-hearted account of his experiences during the holiday expedition to the Italian resort of Rimini, in 1955. Then in Form 5T, he entitled his account:

## *Venimus, Vidimus ...*

"Er, —sidro"

"Sidro?"

"Si, sidro!"

"Non no capito!"

"You know, sidro! – Cider!"

This was the dialogue in a provision store soon after our arrival in Rimini, on Italy's Adriatic coast. Four friends and I had been trying to obtain "sidro" or cider in about six different shops without success. We had been met with blank stares, noncommittal shrugs, or a few words of English interspersed with voluble Italian – but no cider!

But stay! We had reached a shop where a very genial gentleman was most willing to help us. He displayed *Coca–Cola,* fruit cordials, wine and even water. We were driven to making childish drawings of bottles, apples and presses. At last the light dawned and the genial gentleman declared:

"Eet eez eempossible to finda theez sidro 'ere, but perhaps you find eet over there."

*"There"* proved to be a very palatial establishment, resplendent in chromium plating and plastic. We hurried over to this café, bar or drinking parlour, where we were met by an even more cordial gentleman, who spoke English well and told us that he had been to London, where he had many relatives living in the city. With many gesticulations we asked once again. Although very informative, this conversation was not taking us any nearer our objective – *sidro.* Again we asked the barman, who blurted out the terrible truth, apples did not grow in Italy. Therefore there was a marked absence of cider. So in the end we had to content ourselves with *"granite,"* a very good and refreshing substitute, made by pouring fruit essence on finely crushed ice, with soda water added.

The great willingness with which the Italians offered their help to visitors was most impressive. Often it was embarrassing to be the centre of attention; if we merely asked the way a small crowd would gather, each person telling us in Italian his or her opinion as to the best way to get there. Usually someone who could speak English or French would appear to save us at the last moment.

"We were very often asked our nationality at the beginning of a conversation, and Italians often seemed unaccountably disappointed that we were not American".

Apparently driving standards on the Continent were as notorious in those days as they are today. Stan's narrative continues:

"Just how excitable they can be was brought home to us when we were returning by coach from a trip to Rome. We were travelling in a small motor coach whose driver seemed desirous of pushing every other vehicle off the precipitous roads. He never drove at less than 59 mph on the extremely winding mountain roads. Even when he came to a section of the road, which was not metalled, he did not relent, seemingly careless of life or limb. After a while everyone joined in the spirit of the thing, encouraging the driver to go even faster, and cheering madly whenever we passed another coach.

I, and many more of the party would perhaps have many things to say about Italian food – most of them unprintable. *(You have to remember "Pizzahut" and "Caffe Uno" had not appeared at that time! –Ed.)* "It consisted of pasta in very ornate designs – " inner tubes," or "sea shells" and inevitably, olive oil. Nearly every particle of food we ate was thus lubricated; lettuce, tomatoes and

*70*

dandelion leaves. This did not mar our holiday however, for what we lost on the spaghetti, we gained on the *gelati*. There were countless other things to write about; the coffee machines, the kiosk, the primitive sanitation &c. But to describe the trip in full would fill a whole book."

Stan concluded by expressing his and the whole party's gratitude to Mr. Youngs and Mr. Williams for their efficient organisation in making this trip abroad possible.

## Elementary Marine Biology in Pembrokeshire (Or "On Counting Barnacles")

Recorded by Stan Venitt from the July 1956 edition of *The Highburian*

Have you ever tried to count barnacles? Don't! I have, and I regret to say that I failed miserably. I was told to inscribe a two-inch square in chalk on a barnacled rock, and then to count the barnacles within the square, and then by cunning, devious mathematical tricks, to calculate the number of barnacles eking out an existence on the rock. You might think this to be no mean feat, however there was more to come. I was required to distinguish one genus of barnacle from another, and thus prepare a highly technical chart of my observations. To aid me in this Herculean task I was provided with an iron framework measuring one yard by one yard, through which contrivance I was told to gaze. Well, I gazed and saw – barnacles.

This bizarre episode was part of an elementary Marine Biology course at a Field Station at Dale, Pembrokeshire, which a section of the Science sixth attended in October 1955. Besides counting barnacles we graphed seaweed, drew rockpools, and captured numerous shore-dwelling animals, some beautiful, some faintly disgusting and most of them rather smelly. We carried these unfortunate creatures back to the Field centre in jam-jars, and set them out in dishes, fully labelled, to be probed, prodded and examined in minute detail. Finally they met glorious deaths by being thrown over the cliffs into the raging Atlantic below.

We also dug up worms, an altogether nauseating business, for the worms were most retiring in their habits, and had to be forcibly extracted from their despicable burrows or tubes. The most discomfiting habit of the worms is their apparent inability to remain in a solid grippable state whilst being pulled. They merely dissolved into sickening – almost obscene – masses of highly coloured mucilage.

But enough of worms! The Field centre was a romantically situated fort, set on the edge of a cliff. The landscape was remarkably rugged, with rocks, bays, fields, and all the accessories one expects with rugged landscapes. We even braved the elements and went swimming, but the sea was incredibly cold, and our activities were restricted to exercises to restore our circulation.

The highlight of the trip was a visit to Skomer, a small island off the coast. It is completely devoid of human habitation, but there is bird-life enough to satisfy the most avid ornithologist. At great risk to life and limb, we also managed to see a few North Atlantic grey seals.

Most of the day was spent clambering over rocks trying to keep up with the Centre's magnificent warden, who kept us amused with his comments about subjects ranging from Montague's Harriers to wealthy industrialists.

We came away with a heightened respect for the seashore and its inhabitants, excluding those who recline on deck chairs at Southend, newspaper on head, ruminating on fish and chips.

## The School Journey to Wales, Easter 1956

Under the light-hearted guidance of Messrs. Ward and Spurgeon (reported another article in the same edition of the *Highburian Magazine*) twenty-two boys from the Upper School spent five days in Llangollen and two further days in Shrewsbury during the Easter holidays. Under the pretext of gaining extensive geographical knowledge, they all managed to enjoy themselves and keep fully occupied for the whole seven days.

Long uphill walks were endured, and a rich harvest of blisters and aching feet was reaped, along with a sense of pride and mastery after conquering some miniature "Everest." Snowdon was overcome on a cold and threatening day, climbing up the barren rocks in the mist to reach the windy summit at long last, only to descend by no less hazardous a track.

We went from one extreme to another – down a coal mine. Equipped with a miner's safety lamp and helmet we experienced the speedy descent in a lift, and a run through the very bowels of the earth on an electric train to receive a friendly welcome from a Welsh miner both underground and at the pit-head, where much-needed showers were provided.

The days were packed with events: a cold war with a hostel warden, dubbed "Svengali" and his staff; a slide down a scree; our masters caught by the long arm of the law, and the concealment of some of the more riotous members of our group, who habitually staggered in at dead of night via the fire escape.

"Highbury's invasion of Llangollen will long be remembered by the townsfolk, especially by the comely serving wench at a certain café, who suffered the merciless jokes and tricks played by a number of comics to confuse and bewilder her. The boys in their turn will long remember the hectic days spent among the quiet hills and valleys of rural Wales."

# A Visit to Stratford-on-Avon

It was on the last Thursday in June 1956 (reported Malcolm Breckman in *The Highburian* of July 1956) that about 40 boys from all parts of the school met at Paddington Station under the guidance of Messrs. Dennis Ward and Stanley Wood to attend a performance of *Hamlet* at Stratford-on-Avon.

British Railways had provided a special train for the excursion, and had thoughtfully segregated the boys' school from the girls' by allocating them to the central compartments. The journey was otherwise uneventful and we arrived at Stratford at about 12.30 p.m.

As the play was not due to start until 2.30, the party split up into a number of small groups, and set off to explore the town. Some strolled down the wide clean streets, lined with Elizabethan and Jacobean houses, and joined the crowds of tourists visiting famous buildings such as Shakespeare's birthplace, Harvard House, and Anne Hathaway's Cottage. Others preferred to go rowing on the Avon, under the arches of Clopton Bridge and past the Memorial Theatre. Still others passed the time just breathing in the atmosphere of the historic town and its tradition associated with Shakespeare.

Soon it was time for the play, and we assembled at the Memorial Theatre. The play was excellently produced by the Theatre Repertory Company, including Alan Badel, playing Hamlet, Dylis Homlett as Ophelia and Diana Churchill.

When the performance was over we still had time to have a final look at the town, as we strolled along the wide streets back to the station, where our train was waiting to take us back to London, where we arrived at about 9.15 pm. It had been a long, tiring day, but full of pleasant and memorable experiences.

## Trip to the South of France

In 1965 Steve Barrett took part in a school trip to the South of France with Miss Elliott, the buxom French teacher from Ireland and Mr. Myers amongst the accompanying staff members. Miss Elliott went to savour the ambience of France; Mr. Myers to look at Roman ruins. On one of the French trains, a boy in Steve's compartment decided that he no longer wanted the orange juice in a plastic bottle he had with him, and emptied the contents out of the window.

Seconds later an enraged Mr. Myers appeared in their compartment, demanding to know the culprit. Apparently he had been sitting in the next compartment with the window open, and the orange juice had been sucked straight back in through the open window by the air currents, drenching him in the process.

## Swindon and Ford's

Another school trip at about that time was an excursion to the Western Region's Railway locomotive works at Swindon via Paddington, where (*writes Brian Boyle*) we were given a conducted tour around the various heavy engineering workshops. There we were shown locomotives undergoing various stages of dismantling, repair and reassembly, as far as memory now serves me.

Towards the end of my school career, in 1955 I believe, when my thoughts had already begun to turn to learning to drive, I was a keen participant in a school trip to Fords at Dagenham. The visit included the vast furnaces where in those days iron ore was converted into steel, which was then transformed into castings for engines, axles, gearboxes and body panels. The sightseeing tour included the production lines, where the then new 100E series "Anglia" and "Prefect" cars were being produced.

*The covers of* The Highburian Magazine *for July 1953 and June 1964 – the latter lent to us by Bob Remington.*

# Chapter Ten
# *Sporting Highlights*

*Give me the clear blue sky over my head, and the green turf
beneath my feet, a winding road before me, and a three hours
march to dinner – and then to thinking! It is hard if I cannot
start some game on these lone heaths.*

— William Hazlitt, *Table Talk*, 1822

Highbury County School began to establish a proud sporting culture from
its very beginning. An editorial in *The Highburian Magazine* issue of
March 1929 included the following:

"It is with the greatest pleasure that we congratulate both the School elevens
on a most successful season; we have the Captain to tell his own story in
another place. Our only regret is that we have still to enter the Promised Land
of Highams Park. The latest rumour is that the end of March will witness this
long deferred event. In any case we can confidently expect to have our cricket
season there."

## *Football 1929*

"This term's football has been a success for both elevens, and although
influenza was prevalent among some of the players, the results have not been
seriously affected. Team players were:-

1st XI – Warshinsky; Wright, (Matric.), Ritte; Cleaver, Zwich, Montague;
Ferguson, Sleap, Michaels, Stripe and Isherwood.

2nd XI — Wright or Neck; Johnson, Kerr; Smith, Cinnamo, Lack;
Rossomond, Thomas, Green, Flack and Barnett. *(The Wright mentioned
here is the Alfred Arthur Wright, 88 in 2004, who has contributed his own
recollections to this work elsewhere).*

St. IGNATIUS 2 vs H.C.S. 11 – at TOTTENHAM

"Play was fairly even at first, but the School gradually obtained the upper
hand, and scored five goals in the first half. After the interval, St. Ignatius
rallied and netted twice, but deteriorated towards the end, and the School
added six more goals. The scorers were Sleap and Michaels 3, Stripe 2,
Isherwood 1, and 1 own Goal."

HOLLOWAY COUNTY 4 vs H.C.S. 1 at FINCHLEY ...

TRINITY 1 *v* H.C.S. 2 at TRINITY ...

OLD BOYS 6 *v* H.C.S. 2 at SOUTH WOODFORD
"In the first half the Old Boys attacked strongly, and their efforts were rewarded with a goal by Elliot. The School then broke away, and Michaels equalised. The Old Boys attacked again, and another goal was scored by Pearce. In the second half the School attacked strongly at first and Isherwood scored, but afterwards we slackened off and seemed to lack enthusiasm, and left the Old Boys victors by 6 to 2."

H.C.S. 3 *v* GLENDALE 1 at HOME ...

**Criticisms** *(among other players)*
RITTE.— At left back this season he has played excellently throughout, and has been one of the mainstays of our defence. His play against Glendale County on 9th March was outstanding, and he thoroughly deserved the congratulation given by the master of the opposing school.
WRIGHT.— He has been a prominent figure in the defence also, and has a good understanding with his partner Ritte. Together these two backs make a very efficient obstacle for any forwards to overcome.

**Record of Matches Played**

|  |  |  |  | Goals | | |
| P | W | L | D | For | Against | Pts |
| 12 | 7 | 4 | 1 | 67 | 28 | 15 |

Second XI record to date:

| 10 | 7 | 3 | 0 | 55 | 34 |
|----|---|---|---|----|----|

# *Cricket 1939*

*The Highburian Magazine* reported that "this season's cricket has been better than last year's. I venture no reason for that, except that the Removes have provided some new stars. Those 'in the know' forecast that the cricket next year should be better than ever." *(At least those "in the know" did not believe the rumours going around about a War breaking out, then!)*
    "On 29 June the School beat the Parents on the first innings; but they were unable to fulfil their aspirations, which were to dismiss them a second time.

The results bear out the oft-repeated contention that there is plenty of talent in the School, but coaching and practice are needed to bring it to light."

"The First XI started the 1939 season badly. Losing one and drawing the other matches. They did not run into form until their heavy defeat of Leyton County School. Since then our batsmen and bowlers have been in deadly form, and (both) the Parents and Parmiters School have fallen easy prey. It remains to be seen whether the Staff will prove more considerable opponents."

Results:

| | | |
|---|---|---|
| v. | Owens | Match drawn. |
| v. | Monoux | Lost by 8 wickets |
| v. | William Ellis | Match drawn. |
| v. | Holloway | Match drawn. |
| v. | St. Ignatius | Match drawn. |
| v. | Leyton | Won by 10 wickets. |
| v. | Parents | Won by 9 wickets. |
| v. | Parmiters | Won by 8 wickets. |

**The Personnel of the First XI** (criticisms included the following):

R.G. TONGUE, our worthy Captain, is a workmanlike batsman who always seems to turn up trumps when the side most needs his help. It has often been on his broad shoulders that the responsibility of scoring has rested. He is a brilliant fielder, and discharges his duties as Captain with modest efficiency.

G.A. WARNER made a splendid not out 29 in the first match of the season, and then seemed to lose his confidence. He has now, however, redeemed the promise of that innings ... scoring over 100 runs and topping the batting average with 24.2.

B. G. KARAT, Warner's opening partner, has developed a fine forcing style of which a graceful cover drive is the chief scoring stroke – a stroke that is a delight to watch. A tendency to firm-footedness mars his on-side play; when his leg strokes are on a par with his off-play he will be a complete batsman.

O. HILLS. This lad's bowling this season has been an object lesson to all budding bowlers. Concentrating mainly on maintaining an immaculate length, Hills has so far returned the best bowling average of the season (4.53 per wicket). His batting too, especially his cutting, is exhilarating to watch, though it savours somewhat too much of the playground.

A.J.H. PETRE, our fast bowler is the only pace bowler in the side; he thus has to stand up to long unbroken spells, and deserves great praise for his endurance. He has put up some excellent performances; notably 5 wickets for 9 runs (including a hat trick) against Leyton. In the traditional manner of the fast bowler he is capable of some Jim Smith stuff with bat, too.

# Football, 1953

Our sporting chronicle now moves forward to 1953. The war is over and the school long returned from Midsomer Norton (where there were playing fields next door to the classrooms and not a long bus journey away). We are now watching the Highbury First Eleven playing at Highams Park. The school is fielding First, Second and Third Elevens this year, as well as three Under 15 Elevens. *The Highburian Magazine* in its July 1953 Edition commented:

"We regret that lack of space prevents our giving a detailed account of the First Eleven's achievements. They have had a very successful season, which has raised the prestige of the school greatly as regards football. Although we regret losing some very able players, we still have many of our experienced players left, and confidently look forward to another successful season."

## THE FIRST XI PLAYERS FOR THE 1952/3 SEASON

REDDY.—Reliable and safe without being spectacular. He has made splendid progress in the last two years.

SAVIN.— The youngest member of the team. Anticipation extremely sound. He improves with every game he plays.

HANNAM.—Rather slow, but his positional sense has made him reliable and sound.

FIELD.—A good attacking wing half. He has played consistently well.

LOVEJOY.—Has captained the team throughout the season in an extremely capable manner. He has played well and thinks seriously about the game.

PARSONS.—Won his place after three games and has held it ever since, thus showing how much his play has improved. Direct and effective.

DIXON.—He has played some brilliant games, but he must remember that there are ten others in the team. One of the few players who can kick well *with both feet.*

ASHTON.—Lack of ball-control has reduced his effectiveness, but his speed and intelligence have contributed to his being an asset to the side.

ENGLEFIELD.—Rather on the slow side, but opens the game out well and uses his shooting ability whenever possible.

HEX.—Although rather small he has played well, but must try to speed up and be a little more direct.

BARRETT.—A utility player who has filled wing and wing-half positions most efficiently when needed. A very capable reserve.

The full results of all six elevens were as follows:

| | P | W | L | D | Goals For | Against |
|---|---|---|---|---|---|---|
| First XI | 19 | 12 | 2 | 5 | 74 | 33 |
| Second XI | 11 | 1 | 4 | 6 | 21 | 37 |
| Third XI | 1 | 1 | 0 | 0 | 2 | 1 |
| U 15 XI | 2 | 2 | 0 | 0 | 4 | 1 |
| U14 XI | 11 | 3 | 1 | 7 | 28 | 40 |
| U 13 XI | 5 | 0 | 0 | 5 | 4 | 33 |

## *Cricket 1954-55*

In *The Highburian Magazine* July 1955 edition the late Tony Edelstein recorded:

"At the beginning of the season it was thought the School First XI would be fairly strong, and the matches played have justified this view. The play has been entertaining on most occasions, and in only one match did we fail to achieve a definite result. Indeed out of seven matches, we have won four, lost one, drawn one, and in the seventh rain stopped play.

Five members of the side are former first XI players, and these together with newcomers formed a well-balanced side. There is no department of the game in which we are weak this season. The batting and bowling are both up to standard, and the ground fielding is also good, although catches have been dropped at times.

For their fine performances Savin, Seddon, Sandell and White should be mentioned as regards batting, bowling and wicket keeping, but I must again emphasise that our success has been due to teamwork above all. The side has played well together and every member has played his part.

I think that the School XI will do very well in its remaining four matches, and will finish up the season with a great record. In conclusion I would mention that throughout the winter, members of the First XI went to the indoor Cricket School at Alexandra Palace, where we received coaching from the Middlesex County player and Old Boy of our school, Alec Thompson, to whom we are very grateful. I feel that this has contributed in no small measure to our success.

First XI Results
Highbury 85 (Edelstein 31) *v* George Monoux 86 – 6
Stratford 55 (Savin 6 – 8) *v* Highbury 57 – 8
Highbury 101 – 6 decl. (Edghill 39, Sandell 34) *v* Chartsey, 9 (Seddon 5-4, Savin 5-4)

Highbury 93 – 9 decl. *v* Chingford 33 (White 5 – 5)
Highbury 19 – 0 wkt *v* Hackney Downs.
Highbury 135 – 4 decl. (Pingree 53) *v* Staff 40
Highbury 124 – 4 decl. (Savin 73) *v* Leyton County 83– 9.

## Cricket 1956-57

Although we fielded a strong XI, the School has not made a very successful start to the season. The batsmen can put up a hundred runs quite easily and the bowling is sound, yet only one match has been won to date. The weather must be held partly to blame, but also the rather timid batting down the order.

Individually Palmer is a great asset to the team, both with bat and ball, a delightful batsman and a cunning bowler. Savin and Pingree are excellent openers, and the latter scored a brilliant undefeated 63 runs against Minchenden School. Edghill and Wood have also played fine innings, and Seddon maintains a hostile attack with the new ball. Edghill is a popular Captain of an enthusiastic and happy XI, and the Staff may expect to be defeated by a team which must soon follow the winning track.

The School First XI players are: Edghill (Capt.), Savin, Pingree, Palmer, Seddon, Wood, Smith, P. Morecombe, W.K. Elliott, Dickens and Adams. Wilson, Vrahimedes, Sowden, Rawlings and Parr have also been selected.

First XI Results

Highbury 102 – 3 decl. (Savin 46) *v* Quintin 40 – 3
Highbury 61 *v* William Ellis 111 (Palmer 5 – 45)
Highbury 20 – 3 *v* Sir George Monoux 129 (Palmer 6 – 59)
Highbury 64, (Wood 33 n.o.) *v* Stratford 33 – 9 (Palmer 6 – 12)
Highbury 103 – 8 decl. *v* Finchley 104 – 5
Highbury 112 – 1 decl. (Pingree 63 n.o.) *v.* Minchenden 37 (Palmer 4 – 7)
Highbury 82 (Palmer 35) *v* Old Boys 95
Highbury 100 – 7, decl. (Savin 31, Edghill 35) *v* Hackney Downs 66 – 5.
Highbury 114, (Seddon 33) *v* Glendale 29 (Palmer 5 – 8)
Highbury 110, (Seddon 28) *v* Parmiters 56 – 5.

## Football 1954-55

"On the whole the School Football XI has had a reasonable season with fortunes varying at times. After the great success of the previous year, the team had great difficulty trying to emulate the victories of 1953-4. At the start of the season, the inclusion of six new first XI players gave rise to a certain amount of uncertainty throughout the team. The team suffered heavy defeats in the

*The Old Highburians 2nd XI in Belgium, 1957 – Back row: R.Meager, D.Swan, W.Spencer, C.Chandler, L.Peppiatt and A Goodier. Front row: I.Watkins, D.Ireson, V.Downing,R.Mayo and A.Whitehead.*

*The Highbury School First XI, 1955-56 – Back row: M.Wood, A.Dickens, A.Seddon, V.Hyatt, V.Downing and M.Edghill.  Front row: K.Morcombe, P.Savin, G.Hexham, G.Robinson and W.Cram.*

first two games, but then settled down to play very consistently until Christmas.

Mention must also be made of a new fixture, i.e. the Staff versus the School Football XI. Congratulations to the Staff, who unfit as they were, managed to give the School XI a very good and enjoyable game.

At Christmas the School XI lost its goalkeeper, who left school, and once more there was uncertainty in the team. Unfortunately during the second half of the season, the team did not settle down, as the results indicate."

School record until Christmas:

|    |    |    |    | Goals | |
| --- | --- | --- | --- | --- | --- |
| P | W | L | D | For | Against |
| 13 | 8 | 1 | 4 | 54 | 29 |

School record after Christmas:

| 8 | 3 | 1 | 4 | 23 | 34 |

**The School XI players were**:

<pre>
                 Robinson
         Sandell      Tennant
      Field      Savin           Ambrose
  Seddon  White      Hannam   Edghill    Huxham
</pre>

Woodrow, Downing, Stanger and Godfrey also played

## Football 1955-6

So far this season the First XI has played quite well, but heavy scoring by the attack has not been ably supported by a defence which has undergone several changes. The First XI is well on its way to scoring 100 goals (65 at half term), a feat which has never been achieved by the School XI before. The most commendable victories were the 4 – 0 defeat of Owens, a school which the First Team has not beaten for 20 years, and the 10 – 3 victory against Holloway. The other three teams have had a disappointing season, mainly owing to a weak defence.

|  | P | W | L | D | Goals For | Against |
| --- | --- | --- | --- | --- | --- | --- |
| First XI | 13 | 8 | 3 | 2 | 65 | 44 |
| Second XI | 10 | 2 | 8 | 0 | 32 | 49 |
| Under 14s | 11 | 4 | 6 | 1 | 31 | 58 |
| Under 13s | 8 | 3 | 3 | 2 | 33 | 25 |

*The 1953 Highbury School Sports Team*

*The 1954 Highbury School Sports Team – with Captain, Pat Ashton*
*(wearing the Prefect's badge) in the centre of the back row.*

# Athletics and Cross-Country, 1953

"This is the second year of the experiment of spending alternate games days on athletics and cross-country. This experiment was made because of the shortage of pitches at Highams Park, which allowed football or cricket only once a fortnight. Whether or not boys have preferred being chased over Hampstead Heath to an afternoon at their lessons is difficult to say, but some boys have become very keen on this form of sport, and we are slowly pushing our standards up.

"Results in the North London Grammar Schools' Athletics Meeting were very encouraging. The Junior team are to be congratulated on coming fifth out of seventeen schools – a position they earned by their very keen practice and hard work. Of the individuals, Beaumont's first in the mile with a time of 4 minutes 35.8 seconds was outstanding, and Ashton made a gallant attempt in the pole-vault, coming second after very little opportunity for practice. The inter-house cross-country race was run on 24 March, in dry conditions, over a course of approximately three and a half miles on Hampstead Heath. City House gained a clear victory, and Beaumont of City was the first man home."

## "Spotlight on Sport"

*The Highburian Magazine* issue of July 1953 carried the following article, written by Herbert (Zvi) Jagendorf, recently retired as a Professor of English at the Hebrew University, Jerusalem:

There has been a welcome and noticeable spurt in general sports activities in the school this term.

The Rowing Club is going from strength to strength under the efficient and enthusiastic coaching of Mr. Knowles, and we hope to have some really good crews on the river, capable of competing with other rowing schools.

Tennis and badminton are now being played regularly on Wednesday afternoons, and now that the LCC has kindly completed the tennis court in the big playground, we hope that activities will spread throughout the school, and a tournament is in the offing."

At the time of writing (*1953 that is*) the first round of the table-tennis tournament has been played; and to judge by the amount of unofficial practice going on in form rooms, interest is running very high. A school team will be chosen on the results of the tournament, and we shall try to put the school on the London table-tennis map.

The striking innovation this term has been the foundation of the Boxing Club by Mr. Ward, who is an Oxford Blue. It meets in the Gym after school on Mondays and Fridays. A cordial invitation is offered to seniors both with and without experience. May your black eyes be well earned!

*A cross-country at Parliament Hill Fields. Prominent among the judges in the middle photo: Messrs. Knowles, Lincoln, Lane, Davis, Woood and Winter. Bottom photo: Messrs. Laurie, Howells, Rosenthal, Lewis, Golding, Leech and Taylor.*

*The Highbury School Sports Team, 1956*

*The Highbury School Under-15s team which was beaten 0–1 by Holloway School in the final of the Islington Gazette Cup, 1965 – Back row: Hooper, Avery, Taylor, Hutchins, Simpson and Chillingworth. Front row: Chryssalis, Gregory, Fuschillo, Davey and James.*

*STOP PRESS:* No fewer than five of this year's 1ˢᵗ XI have been chosen to play in the N.London *v* S.London Grammar Schools Match, from which players will be chosen to represent the whole of London. They are the following: Reddy (Goalkeeper), Savin (centre-half), Field (right half), Dixon (inside forward), and Edghill (inside forward). We hope to see other members of the School XI joining Dixon in the Londoners' side this season.

## *House Notes*

### CANONBURY

*December 1953:* "We had a moderately successful cricket season; the Juniors are to be congratulated on sharing first place in the championship table with City. The Seniors did not fare so well, but next season new blood will make some difference to the team. The Senior Football team has fared very well so far, and the Juniors can be relied upon to do likewise. We expect our cross-country team to do great things this time, and we hope that every member of the House will take an interest in its activities, and so help put Canonbury house back on top."

*July 1955:* "Although finishing third in the School Sports, the House gave a good account of itself, and was compensated by the closeness of the result. Congratulations to Finsbury House for winning the Sports, and thereby ending a run of victories by City House, and to Hyatt for gaining the junior "Victor Ludorum" The House also finished third in the Cross-country Championship, the individual title going to Robert Thomas, the Captain of our cross-country team. The House Football XI played very well considering the fact that many of our players were selected from the Junior School. We would have liked to confine selection to the Seniors, but there is unfortunately a scarcity of players here. Nevertheless, the experience gained should be of advantage to those Juniors who played, during the coming season." B. FIELD, (CAPT.)

*January 1956:* In *The Highburian Magazine* for this month R.W.J. (Ron) Wilson was Canonbury House correspondent, and filed this report:

"Canonbury has not had a good season. There appears to be lack of House spirit among the senior members. In the senior six-a-side football Canonbury were well beaten by City, only five turning out. The junior side also lost in the opening round, but the middle side reached the final, being narrowly beaten by City. Although Canonbury did not win a cup in the Swimming Gala, they did very well, gaining the highest number of overall points. In the football games the Senior and Junior teams have lost their games, while the middle side, playing excellent football, have won all their games against the other Houses."

## CITY

*December 1953:* "Last year was a very successful one for us, and on Speech Night Pat Ashton was presented with the Cock House Cup for the third time in succession. We tied for top place in both the Senior and Junior cricket championships, and were disappointed that the sports were cancelled (due to the weather), especially as we were confident that with the cross-country victory behind us, we were confident of another win."

*July 1955:* "So far this year we have two cups to our credit, the Cross-country and the Senior Football Cups. We were rather unlucky in the School Sports, which were the most thrilling we have seen for some time at Highbury, when we were beaten by Finsbury, by the narrow margin of 2½ points. Whereas our Senior Football team was placed first in the Senior competition, unfortunately our Juniors were placed last in the Junior contest. On the whole our Seniors had a much more successful season than the Juniors, but we hope the Juniors will do better next year, for they will be the ones that the House will have to rely on in the future. Well, here's looking forward to a brighter year!" P. SAVIN

*January 1956:* "Once again we can congratulate ourselves on winning the Cock House Cup. The senior cricket XI won all its matches by a large margin, but the juniors, despite gallant efforts, did not fare so well. In the Swimming Gala the House was not as keen as in other sports, and as a result no improvement was made on last year's poor showing. This was fully compensated for, however, in the six-a-side tournament, where the senior, middle and juniors all won their respective sections after some hard-fought games. So far the junior and senior XIs are undefeated in the House competition, and without too much optimism we may hope to add to our previous successes."

## FINSBURY

*December 1953:* "This has not been one of our successful cricket years, despite the Captain of the School XI also being Captain of the House Senior XI. Both House teams finished third in the tables, but we are confident that this will be put right next season. The School football Captain, K. Dixon, will certainly lead the Finsbury team to victory this season. Dixon was chosen to play for London Grammar Schools last year, and has been chosen this year to play in the North vs. South Trial match already."

*July 1955:* "Congratulations must be given to all members of Finsbury House who contributed to our success in the sporting activities of this year. A good start was made in the Swimming Gala, held at the beginning of the School year, when our Senior team, captained by Busley of 5T, won the Senior swimming trophy. This was followed by the good performance of our cross-country team, which was placed second to City House in the annual Cross-country Race. The House Football XI too, did well in drawing two of its matches, those against Stoke (5–5), and Canonbury (3–3). Our final position at the end of the season was third. There is little doubt that our outstanding achievement was the very fine win on Sports Day, when we narrowly, but convincingly defeated City House." J. W. AMBROSE

*January 1956:* "Although we had a moderately successful season, we hope to benefit greatly from the more frequent House meetings that are now held. We are pleased to see that most of our seniors, and not the usual minority, contributed to winning the Senior Swimming Cup. The seniors reached the final of the six-a-side, but were beaten narrowly by a strong City team. The juniors and middles have not fared so well either in the swimming or the six-a-side and eleven-a-side football, however in athletics they are more promising than the seniors."

### STOKE

*December 1953:* "The school year hardly seemed complete without Sports Day, which had to be cancelled due to the bad weather this year. The House was far more successful on the cricket field than in the football season. We tied with City for top place in the Senior table, and supplied half of the players in the School First XI for most of the season. Edelstein, Reddy, Day, Shapiro and Morrison played for the First XI against the Masters XI."

*July 1955:* "This has been quite a successful year for the House. In the first event of the School year, the Swimming Gala, Stoke took first place in the Junior event and came second in the Senior one. Batt must be congratulated on winning the "Victor Ludorum" (Swimming). In the six-a-side football we came first in the Middle and were runners-up in the Junior section. I should like to congratulate the Juniors on a fine all round performance this year, especially as the Seniors did not come up to the expected standard. With our present Juniors we can look forward to many successful years in all fields of sport." TONY EDELSTEIN.

*January 1956:* "For the second year in succession our main success was in the Swimming Gala, winning the Junior House Cup and all three relays. Our football teams have played well, but owing to the absences of some of our key players, we have had no success. All three of our six-a-side teams suffered defeats, as did the other Houses against the supremacy of City. This year's Sports Day was a disappointment after last year's effort, although as always, our House has outstanding individuals. The main fault of the House is not the lack of individual ability, but the apathy shown by most of the House." PETER LOWE.

## Chapter Eleven
# An ABC of Clubs and Societies

We have looked in some detail at the programme of seasonal sporting activities in which most of the boys participated with varying degrees of enthusiasm at Higham's Park, Parliament Hill and other venues over the years. The boys were also encouraged to involve themselves in a wide range of other activities both in and outside school. Browsing through old editions of *The Highburian Magazine* illustrates how varied these were. In July 1954 we read of the Rowing Club Regatta, The Easter Concert by the Choir, The School Quiz, the Tuck Shop, the Debating Society, the Photographic Society, and a new Society, which introduced the boys to comparative Religions. The following will no doubt prompt recollections among readers of participation in these and other events.

**A is for Air Training Corps Squadron.** Douglas Hague (1937-1940) belonged to this prior to joining the RAF. He says the officer in charge was Mr. Wood and the other officer Mr. Dorrington.

**A is for Aero-Modelling**. Early in 1956 a Fourth former and some enterprising Lower Sixth formers started an aero-modelling Club, meeting after school on Fridays. With Field as organiser, and Marcus Burstin as Treasurer, the club was soon able to repay a loan from Mr. King. Although numbers were small, a Sunday trip to Epsom Downs was planned to try out some of the models they had constructed.

**A is also for Army Cadet Force**. The Highburian Magazine for March 1929 reported: "Up to the time of going to print there have been few parades in which "D" Company has been represented. At the end of last year the Boxing Competition was fought at St. Agatha's Hall, adjoining Headquarters. Our boys had a strong entry, and carried off the Shield by a comfortable margin of points. "C" Company were placed second. Though most of the senior cadets of our Company who entered were beaten either before, or in the Finals, the juniors did extremely well, and gained most of our points. A junior officer of another battalion presented the prizes to the winners at the end of the evening."

Marathon Cup, 1929: "This cup was competed for on the 24 February at Chingford, over a five-mile course. Our company was represented by seven runners who, after a very close race, were placed second, the Buglers beating us by 9 points to 70. This was a very good performance considering the condition of the ground and the respective ages of our runners and those of the Buglers. Under the skilful supervision of Lieut. Gage our gymnastic display for the coming Battalion prize distribution is progressing favourably. Signed Cpl. Montague and Cpl. McCullough.

**A is also for Athletics**. In 1952 the School began an experiment of spending alternate games days on athletics and cross-country running. Due to the shortage of pitches at Highams Park football or cricket could only be played every two weeks. *The Highburian Magazine* in July 1953 recorded: "It is difficult to say whether or not the boys have preferred being chased over Hampstead Heath to an afternoon at their lessons, but some boys have become very keen on this sport, and we are pushing our standards up slowly. Next year we are hoping for more pitches at Highams Park, so rather different arrangements will be tried. Results in the North London Grammar Schools' Athletics Meeting were very encouraging. The Junior team are to be congratulated on coming fifth out of seventeen schools – a position they earned by their very keen practice and hard work." ... "Beaumont's first in the mile with a time of 4 minutes 35.8 seconds was outstanding."

The actual Athletics Club was set up in 1956 with the object "to create an interest in athletics, and interest has been sadly lacking". An article in the July 1957 edition of the magazine – signed by Sixthformers D.T. Weldon and B. Travis – explained that the problem was not a lack of talent at Highbury or lack of enthusiasm among masters, but lack of time devoted to training. "The modern athlete cannot reach his peak on one afternoon's training a week; and games are limited to one afternoon a week. So the Athletics Club was formed to devote Saturday mornings to serious training."

**B is for Badminton**: In *The Highburian Magazine* of July 1955, R.E. Oughton, Badminton Club correspondent, reported:

"The Club has been in existence for some years now, and has produced several players of more than average ability. Indeed one of its past members, *Baker* is now a Cambridge Half Blue in Badminton. It is only recently however, have we played matches with other clubs. After our initial successes in beating *St. Mary's* and *Holloway County*, we look forward confidently to games against *Hackney Downs* and *William Ellis*. Our eagerly awaited match *the Masters versus Boys* game, now seems unlikely to be held this year, due either to the reluctance or inability of the Masters to form a team for the occasion. The Club meets on alternate Friday evenings; extra practice is also allowed on Games afternoons. The Subscription is 3d. per session, covering the cost of the school's rackets and shuttlecocks. *(Yes, threepence in old money!)* Tea is also available for luxury-seekers. Although club membership is limited to the sixth form and a certain number of fifth-formers, we hope that this article may have interested some of the younger boys sufficiently for them to look forward to becoming eligible for membership."

The *Highburian Magazine* edition of July 1954 carried the report of a very successful season for the Old Highburians Badminton League Team, who had won four of the five matches played in Division Five of the Middlesex Badminton Association. If they could manage to win the only League match still to play, there was every likelihood of promotion in the following season. The Knock-out Competition team had survived the first round for the first time for four years, to reach the semi-final, in which they were beaten 2 – 7 by Cazenove Badminton Club. However the result was no disgrace for the Old Boys, as their opponents team included several County players, and had won the competition five times since 1945.

The Old Boys had won three of the seven friendly matches also played, providing excellent opportunities for match practice to members who had as yet not been selected for the first Team, including Brian Youngs, a promising new recruit from the school.

In its July 1956 edition *The Highburian Magazine* also carried a Report from the Old Boys Badminton Section. After their promotion in the previous year they had enjoyed a reasonably successful season, winning 11 of the 17 matches played, to finish as runners-up in Division 4A. Their best performance in the League had been a resounding home victory by six rubbers to three over the Polytechnic 3rd Team, who eventually topped the Division.

In the Middlesex Knock-Out Cup the Old Boys survived the second round – after a "bye" in the first – only then to be well and truly beaten by the "Penguins."

**B is also for Boxing.** The same issue carried a report by J. Holder of 5E on the activities of the Boxing Club. "The Boxing Club has met with considerable success since it was formed by Mr. Dennis Ward a few years ago. Our first contest was against Holloway County last November, when we won by eight bouts to four, and a draw 7-7. However on the same evening Godfrey and Southon won two special bouts against Holloway. In the Inter-Schools Championships Cardozo gained an Islington Championship, Godfrey gained a North London Championship, and Southon a North West London Championship. Merino became a London Champion in the same contest. He was unfortunately beaten on points when he boxed in the All England Championship.

"In the autumn term we hope to continue the contests with other schools, and to enter some of our boys again in the Inter Schools Championships. Training is held in the Gym after school on Thursdays." In the 1956 Schoolboy Championships Southon won the award for the most stylish boxer, and became London Champion. He was unfortunately unable to box in the next round of the competition. Ken Cardozo reached the semi-finals, and Green won the Islington championship. The Club was able to demonstrate its supremacy in the two triangular tournaments with Holloway County and Woodberry Downs.

**C is also for cross-country**. In April 1954 the Inter House cross-country Race was held at Parliament Hill Fields, and reported in the Magazine's July edition.

"It was a fine April afternoon, and the ground underfoot was very firm as the teams gathered at the foot of the steep hill, and Mr. King started the race. Despite the favourable conditions, many had predicted that this year's race would be very slow, as there was no exceptional runner who would force the pace. From the start however, a group of about fifteen forged ahead, but before long this break away group had dwindled to about six. Several runners had determined that *Herbert,* who had already won the mile and the half-mile in the School Sports, would not complete the hat-trick by winning the cross-country as well. After about a mile first one, then another group were seen sprinting ahead.

"*Pilcher* stormed ahead over the section of the course that passes through the woods, and their job was done. *Herbert* was out of the race, but *Pilcher* had burnt himself out in the process. It now seemed certain that the race would be won by one of the first four, who stayed well together until the Tea-House, when *Bucks* and *Wilkes* sprinted ahead. It was touch and go which of this pair would win, but *Wilkes* eventually managed to be first past the post."

The 1954 School sports were held at Parliament Hill Fields, Hampstead for the first time, having been held at the end of the Summer Term at Highams Park, Walthamstow in previous years. This change brought about improved times and performances by all; sixteen records were broken and two were equalled. Although the weather was rather cold, the sun did put in an appearance at the finals. Right up to the last race, the keener competition left the possibility open for an alteration in the positions of the Houses. The final positions were Canonbury 157 points, City 174 points, Finsbury 137 points and Stoke with 148 points. On finals day Canonbury scored a further 72 points, City a further 60 points, Finsbury another 48 points and Stoke another 67 points. Pat Ashton of City House won the Senior Victor Ludorum Cup, while Fantham of Stoke won the Junior Victor Ludorum. The Sports Trophy for the Winning House was presented to Pat Ashton by the Chairman of the Governors.

**D is for Dancing Class**. Ballroom Dancing Classes were held on weekday evenings in the School Hall for boys in the Remove and upwards, sponsored by the Parents' Association. These were also promoted to the girls of Highbury Hill School, to provide the necessary partners. The dancing classes were thus very popular and well attended.

There we learned the social graces of a smart turn-out – jeans, tee-shirts, crop tops and mini-skirts were still in the future – combing one's hair, disposing of one's chewing gum before asking a young lady for "the pleasure of the next dance" was *de rigueur* and making polite conversation was encouraged.

The instructor, Eric and his wife or fiancée, taught us the intricacies of the waltz, quickstep, foxtrot, samba and a very trendy jive, cha-cha-cha and samba, with such refinements in performance as the "hesitation," "fishtail" and reverse turn. If memory serves, there was also something called "The Creep," which involved a shuffling step, holding one's partner in a tight embrace, while wearing a "one-button drape" jacket with an imitation velvet collar, narrow "stove-pipe" trousers and thick crepe-soled shoes. The fashionable hair-style was the "Tony Curtis" quiff, and the D.A. A valuable – if incidental – lesson also to be learnt, was in handling rejection, after taking a long time to summon the pluck to invite a young lady to dance in the first place.

We danced our "slow-slow-quick-quick-slow" steps to popular music on shellac records recorded by Victor Sylvester *et al.*, played on a gramophone. We held our partners at a respectful arm's length, with a simple, naïve pleasure, fuelled only by soft drinks, provided for a mere few pence (in pre-decimal currency) by the Parents' Association. Once one's two left feet had acquired sufficient rhythm and sense of direction to avoid trampling on a girl's feet, one was encouraged to attend the Parents' Association monthly dances. These used to be held on a Saturday evening in the School Hall, for which the admission price was about 2/- i.e. two shillings.

From this training ground one could demonstrate one's social skills at Town Hall Dances in Islington, Finsbury, Stoke Newington or St. Pancras. From these one could graduate to the Hammersmith Palais, the Streatham Locarno or the Lyceum in the West End.

**D is also for the Debating Society**, which was formed during the Spring Term of 1954, met every week until the start of the Examinations. The attendance of only a dozen or so enthusiastic members did not do justice to the highly controversial subjects discussed. So controversial were they indeed that the house witnessed the forceful expression of the views of many members simultaneously. Among the causes of such emotion were the debate on Polygamy and a discussion on Communism. There were also debates on Commercial Television and German Rearmament, also a most instructive talk on Buddhism.

Another activity of the Society had been a periodic meeting called *The Critics* in which members prepared a critique of a book, a film and a radio programme. A mock trial of the Prefects was in course of preparation, and was expected to produce "some quite startling revelations." Membership was restricted to fifth and sixth formers, but consideration was being given to extending the privilege to the Removes.

**E is for Easter Concert**. These Concerts were a tradition going back to the School's earliest days. Here for instance is the report from *The Highburian* July 1954.

"This year's Easter Concert upheld the high standard of previous years, due mainly to the energetic conducting by Mr. Taylor, with excellent piano accompaniment from Mr. Lincoln. The choir was augmented by a handful of girls from Highbury Hill, some Old Boys and parents. Two items in particular drew prolonged applause from the audience: Handel's Coronation anthem *Zadok the Priest*, and the Bach Chorale, *Jesu Joy of Man's Desiring*. The Concert did not consist only of classical works however. The music, ranging from a Negro spiritual to a skit on a nursery rhyme had a universal appeal."

**F is for Film Society.** Organised by Mr. S.B. Davis (as mentioned earlier in the book by George Cobby) the Film Society (or Cinema Club) met in a room that many people in school knew nothing about – up the passage beyond the swimming pool. Notable successes were *Battleship Potemkin, The History of Mr. Polly* (from the H.G. Wells novel some of us were reading for O Level) and of course the Charlie Chaplin and Marx Brothers films which Steve Davis liked so much. In *The Highburian Magazine* for December 1953, Malcolm Breckman wrote that the price of admission of 5d. for members and a shilling for non-members was very reasonable in view of the cost of film hire. The autumn term began with the *49th Parallel* playing to a full house – "the film itself was another of those war stories, but it was enjoyable in spite of that." Malcolm's complaint was his inability to distinguish one voice from another because of the lack of contrast in the speakers.

**G is for Geographical Society.** This society had a most active programme in 1939, with visits to Epping Forest, Watford, Caterham, the Geological Museum and London Docks – 80 boys went on a river trip with Messrs. Bull and Marshall, visiting the Royal Victoria and King George V docks, where they saw the RMS Dunbar Castle which ran an express service to Cape Town, and the Dominion Monarch, the world's largest motor-ship.

**G is also for Gramophone Club.** The July 1953 magazine appealed for suggestions – for, although the last meeting had featured Beethoven, Mendelssohn, Sibelius and Schumann, it was not intended to be a classical music club. A varied programme was needed for the Tuesday dinner time meetings. Suggestions should go to Wilkes or Reddy. This was in the days of 78 rpm shellac discs, of course, and the school possessed a gramophone with an automatic changer, which dropped each one of a stack of half a dozen discs — vinyl L.P.s (33 rpm) came in later.

**L is for Literary and Debating Society**: The March 1929 Highburian reported that the society was experimenting with new activities – a political debate (at the end of which "the Conservative Government was upheld by a small majority") and the techniques of radio drama, members speaking from behind an illuminated silk screen.

**M is for Music Club.** The Music Club was started in 1955 with the aim of interesting the boys in Classical Music, with support of Mrs. Gauld, who loaned the group most of the records for their programmes. The Club was open to everybody from first years to Sixth formers. Members were invited to bring their own records, whether Gigli or Johnnie Ray, The London Philharmonic Orchestra or Ray Ellington Quartet, providing a week's notice of their choice was given. Interest had waned by the following year however, perhaps because they had been able to hold relatively few meetings. In an effort to win a wider appeal, it was pointed out that the greater the variety of music played, the more enjoyable the meetings could be, and members had brought along several jazz records to meetings. If sufficient interest were shown it was hoped that visits to the Royal Festival Hall and Covent Garden Opera House could be arranged.

This Club probably failed to survive when its main proponent, and *Highburian Magazine* correspondent, Ray Oughton, left school that year.

**Q is for Quizzes.** The following reports appeared in *The Highburian*:
The final of the 1954 Islington Schools' Quiz was held at Islington Town Hall on Tuesday 13th April. In this contest we were competing with Tudor Girls' School. The event was well supported and the Town Hall was filled. The School Team members were: Brian Boyle (captain), D. Barry, E. Cross, J.H. Field, A. Kerron and A. Thorncroft. From the start we drew ahead, and as the contest progressed, our lead increased. It was an excellent contest with high scores on each side; the final scores were Tudor Girls 69, Highbury County 81.

The School Regatta in 1954 featured a fours race between the footballers and the masters. Above: the footballers prepare to start with Hannam, Reddy and Ashton steadying their oars.

Left: an enthusiastic Mr. Knowles shows the staff how to pull for victory. The heads in the foreground are said to represent Messrs. Youngs and Ward.

Mr. King found himself in the happy position of being the Headmaster of the winning schools for two successive years. He had been the Headmaster of Holloway County when they won the previous year. The Mayor of Islington presented the cup to our captain.

The following year the contest took place at the Town Hall on 28 March. Highbury County retained the Cup by defeating a team from Laycock Secondary. Although the Laycock team did manage to draw up to within 15 points at one time, the outcome of the contest was never in any doubt. The Highbury County team, John Field, (Capt.), D. Barry, M. Freeman, P. Smith, A. Thorncroft and R. Trickey, won finally by 88½ points to 58½. The Mayor, Ald. Mrs. J.M. Barnes, presenting the silver cup to John Field, remarked on the Headmaster's third successive year as holder of the trophy, and commiserated with the gallant losers.

**R is for Round Table**. The Round Table Society was another short-lived venture. Formed in 1955 by a group of Sixth formers, and continued in 1956 by others, it began by asking visiting guest speakers to give a short talk on such varied topics as "History as a means of Culture," "What is Theosophy?" and "Film: Art or Industry?" In the first year attendances were good, and the meetings were successful. Perhaps the successors lacked the founder's talents, but latterly the audiences showed no active interest in the topics when questions were invited.

**R is for Rowing**. The 19 June 1954 gave a glorious, sunny afternoon for the Under-16 Regatta, organised by the Thames Tradesmen Rowing Club at Mortlake. The Rowing Club had a very successful day at the Regatta. Two crews were entered in the Tub Fours event, one of which was three times unbeaten, to win the first Trophy the Club has brought home. The few spectators had a most enjoyable time, especially in the last race which, after several changes of position, was won by half a length. Both crews fully deserved their success, having put a lot of hard work into the preparations for this Regatta, and the way in which they responded to the enthusiasm of Mr. Knowles. Well done, the Rowing Club!

**S is for Scientific Society.** In May 1939 the society was treated to a fictional film portraying the invention of the pneumatic tyre – produced by the Dunlop Company.

## Chapter Twelve
# The Highbury School Dramatic Society

*If it be true that 'good wine needs no bush',*
*'tis true that a good play needs no epilogue.*
*As You Like It,* Shakespeare.

Each December from the school's earliest years, the Highbury School Dramatic Society (to give it its later name) put on a play. And the staff and cast always aimed at the very highest standards of acting, scenery and costumes. Anyone who took part in one of the annual plays will confirm that getting a part or a role backstage was by no means a rest cure. David Perman recalls having his Cockney vowels beaten out of him (quite literally) when D.C. Leech gave him a part in *The Duke in Darkness*.

A complete list of all the Highbury productions may not be possible. But here are those that are recorded in *The Highburian Magazine*, the local newspapers and surviving play programmes:

| | | |
|---|---|---|
| 1928 | The Devil's Disciple | George Bernard Shaw |
| 1929 | The Mob | John Galsworthy |
| 1930 | The Great Adventure | Arnold Bennett |
| 1931 | R.U.R. | Karel Capek |
| 1932 | Badger's Green | R C Sheriff |
| 1933 | A. Applejohn's Adventure | Walter Hackett |
| 1934 | Abraham Lincoln | John Drinkwater |
| 1935 | Seven Keys to Baldpate | G M Cohan |
| 1936 | Strife | John Galsworthy |
| 1937 | Youth at the Helm | H Griffith |
| 1938 | Libel | Edward Wooll |
| 1947 | Frozen Glory | Sewell Stokes |
| 1948 | Noah | André Obey |
| 1949 | Arsenic and Old Lace | J Kesselring |
| 1950 | Winslow Boy | Terence Rattigan |
| 1951 | The Duke in Darkness | Patrick Hamilton |
| 1952 | The Guinea-Pig | Warren Chetham-Strode |
| 1953 | Morning Departure | Kenneth Woollard |
| 1954 | Worm's Eye View | R F Delderfield |
| 1955 | Major Barbara | George Bernard Shaw |
| 1956 | Home at Seven | R C Sherriff |
| 1964 | Tartuffe | Molière |

This is by no means an exhaustive list of Highbury dramatic productions. Douglas Hague, who attended Highbury County from September 1937 until mid-1940 (he was one of those who returned to Islington just in time for the Blitz) sent us the programme of a performance in late 1944 or early 1945. It was a joint venture by Highbury County and Highbury Hill Girls' School, going under the name of "Highbury Theatre Group". The performance, in the Islington Central Library, Holloway Road, consisted of *Deidre,* a short play by W.B. Yeats, and four scenes from Act IV of Shakespeare's *Macbeth.* The plays were produced by Sydney Williams, the scenery built by James Fowles and songs were arranged by Leslie Lincoln (as ever). The whole performance was in aid of the Highbury County Old Boys Comforts Fund. And not all the plays were stand alone performances. In 1928 George Bernard Shaw's play, *The Devil's Disciple*, was performed as the second half of the Prize Distribution in the large hall of the Northern Polytechnic. The play replaced any speech by the visiting bigwig (in this case the Mayor of Islington) which must have pleased some of the audience. However, it would have been a long evening.

The 1951 school play, *The Duke in Darkness*, was an intensely heavy play. Although the acting was quite up to its usual standard, such a play was too much for a school dramatic society and indeed for a school audience. At least this was the view expressed by Blumenthal and Page at the start of their review of the successful 1952 production of *The Guinea Pig* by W. Chetham-Strode for *The Highburian Magazine.*

*The Duke in Darkness – left to right: Herbert Jagendorf, Anthony Barwick, Patrick Ashton, Alan Shapiro kneeling at the feet of Gary Pearson as the Duke, Fred Reddy, Alan Woodard, David Perman, Alfred Dance and David Abrahams.*

The 1952 production, *The Guinea Pig* consisted of two interwoven plots, depicting life in a Public School as completely opposite to life at Highbury County. The main theme tells of the trials and hardships of the son of a Walthamstow tobacconist in adapting to a Public School environment in which a young master, new to the school, champions him. The "guinea pig", Read, is granted an experimental scholarship to Saintbury, a Public School, by the progressive Board of Education. The boy's inability to adapt plays a large part in the uneasiness of his situation. If he succeeds, the scheme at Saintbury succeeds and the faith put in both of them by the Headmaster, Stringer, will be vindicated.

The secondary theme is the struggle which the "die-hard reactionary" Housemaster, Hartley, has with the progressive policy and with the liberal-minded new master, Lorraine. A love affair between Lorraine and the Housemaster's daughter, Lynne Hartley, is added for good measure. In an excellent performance as Hartley, Herbert Jagendorf commanded the stage with his forceful voice and actions, and Anthony Barwick was utterly convincing in the role of Nigel Lorraine. The part of Read was sympathetically acted by Patrick Hartigan, who showed his wide range of ability as the two different Reads. The female roles were well portrayed by Roger Robinson as Mrs. Hartley, Alan Lipton as Lynne Hartley and Malcolm Breckman as Mrs. Read,

*Above: The cast of "The Guinea-Pig" – Back row: Anthony Barwick, David Fenn, David Perman, Alan Shapiro, Patrick Hartigan and Malcolm Breckman. Front row: Peter Lewins, Alan Lipkin, Herbert Jagendorf, Roger Robinson and John Taylor. Below: A tense moment in the play, when Herbert Jagendorf (left) as Hartley confronts Anthony Barwick as Nigel Lorraine (far right).*

the boy's mother. Also outstanding in the cast were David Perman as Mr. Stringer, the Headmaster, and Alan Shapiro as the Walthamstow tobacconist, Mr. Read. The audience, who was absorbed in the smooth running of the plot and the acting against an excellent setting, were well entertained. This was to be Mr. Donald Leech's last production before his retirement.

## Morning Departure, 1953

Mr. Stanley Wood took over production for the Dramatic Society's December 1953 presentation of Kenneth Woollard's *Morning Departure*. The play is a difficult one to present; for the action is distributed between the main set in the interior of the submarine and various offices ashore, and the rapid changes of scene are exacting. The idea of representing the offices by small cubicles equipped with telephones was good; but the lack of space brought limitations. On the whole, however, the setting and planning were excellent – Messrs. Beverton and Ward assisted Mr. Wood in the production and HSDS made its own scenery, under the direction of Messrs. Lane and Laurie.

The play was well cast – according to a review by Stan Vennitt in *The Highburian Magazine* of July 1954. David Perman was admirable as the "skipper" of the stricken submarine; and Donald Brown was suitably commanding as his "Number One." Patrick Hartigan as Lt. McFee, the Scottish Engineering Officer, gave one of the best performances; his convincing Scottish accent never once faltered throughout. Tom Johnson as Stoker Snipe, the unfortunate

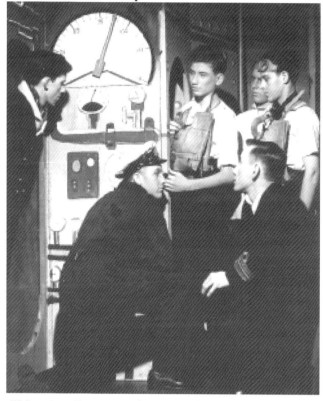

*"Morning Departure"* – *(standing) Donald Brown, Joe Glasberg, Anthony Sandell and Tom Johnson; (kneeling) Patrick Hartigan and David Perman.*

seaman who suffers from claustrophobia and breaks his arm, acted the role excellently. Tony Sandell played Higgins, the Cockney mess steward, extremely well – although his frequent flick-of-the-wrist gestures were sometimes irritating. The officers ashore were all well portrayed: Brian Boyle, Herbert Jagendorf, Alan Lipton and Robert Thomas kept the tension of the rescue operations at a high pitch, through portrayal of a studied clash of personalities.

The "effects" deserve special mention. The sound of water rushing in to fill the escape chamber was terrifyingly realistic. The "chlorine gas', however was rather too realistic; for it also enveloped the first few rows of the audience. Fortunately the inevitable limitations did little to detract from what must be considered an excellent production.

In the same issue are a review by the late Robert Thomas of the play *Refund*, performed by the Remove in conjunction with the Easter Concert; also "The Remove Play" by G. James of the Remove; an article taking a humorous look behind the scenes on the opening night:

"The Remove play was a happier choice than in former years, (wrote Robert Thomas), *Refund* was well within the capabilities of the Removes and gave them the chance to imitate the personal peculiarities of some staff members. In his speech during the interval Mr. King remarked that for the past few weeks Remove formers had been taking note of every movement made by masters during their lessons. The producers, Mr. Beverton and Mr. Ward were to be congratulated, both on their choice of play, and on the skill with which they had licked the cast into shape."

## The Remove Play, 1954

Gaggles of nervous youths have muffed many lines upon the stage at Highbury for the sake of the legitimate theatre, but never so often as when the Remove boys put on a play at Easter. Let us now enter the dressing room on that fateful night of the presentation of *Refund*. In one corner Burstin has realised the magnitude of the thing and has given way to incoherent mutterings. Carter sits helplessly overawed, caught up by a fear greater than he had anticipated. James stirs uneasily under about half a hundredweight of crepe hair. Blitstein, Burt and Watson are playing poker listlessly, but their hearts are not in it; they are imagining themselves out there on stage, having all forgotten their lines. Watson ad-libs by singing "I've got a Lovely Bunch of Coconuts," and switches to "Ave Maria," but too late; the audience rushes the stage…"

"You're next!" Watson staggers to the make-up chair. Burt throws down his hand in disgust. Litman announces to the company in general that he really has forgotten his lines. This amuses the make-up expert, who is seized upon by five members of the cast, who are longing to release pent up emotions.

"It's nothing to laugh at, you ass!"

"Fancy thinking that's funny!"

"I don't think much of the way you've done my make-up!"

"Nor mine!"

"Nor mine!"

The make-up artist subsides, defeated. Enter the Producer.

"Everything all right?" The question is received with bitter laughter. The producer is disconcerted.

"Oh well, you're on in ten minutes."

"Ten minutes? But I'm not even made up yet! I can't go on looking like this!"

But by the time the ten minutes are up, the scenery has been erected and the actors are all ready and correct. Litman and Blitstein are on, and lines that were received in stony silence at rehearsals actually make the audience laugh. Behind the scenery the rest of the cast listens and watches through holes made by a stagehand. The actors have been given their cues; they enter through doors, which seem ready to collapse; as the lights hit them in the face, their make-up runs into their eyes. Litman finds that his moustache isn't such a nuisance after all. Carter manages to walk across stage without collapsing with laughter. Although the prompter seemed not to want to have anything to

*The cast of the Remove play, "Refund", line up with producers Dennis Ward and Ronald Beverton at either end, and stage manager Bill Laurie in the middle.*

do with the sordid business of prompting, the play went with a swing, and all too soon it was over. The cast retires to the dressing room and congratulates one another. After removing our make-up we all go home, while visions of the Old Vic are still fresh.

## Worm's Eye View, 1954

Writing in the July edition of The Highburian Magazine, Stan Vennitt concluded that "this year's production of R.F. Delderfield's *Worm's Eye View*, which had such a phenomenal run at the Whitehall Theatre, made a welcome break with tradition." The action of the play is set in a dingy billet in a small seaside town somewhere in the Midlands. The proprietress, Mrs. Bounty is a hard-bitten shrewish woman, who rules her husband with a rod of iron, and whose superiority complex is rooted in her conceited stepson's position in local government. George James ably portrayed this hatchet-faced dragon.

Alfred Burt gave a most convincing performance as Sydney Spooner, whose exaggerated manner as a pompous petty despot was wholly in keeping with the part. In particular, he domineered Bella, the daughter, outstandingly acted by David Barrett, who captured Bella's timid manner wonderfully.

Billeted on the Bounty "menage" were a group of high-spirited amorous airmen: Porter, the Cockney racketeer; "Pop," the veteran; "the Duke," a typical

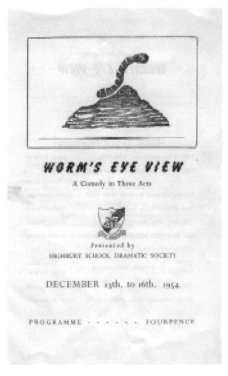

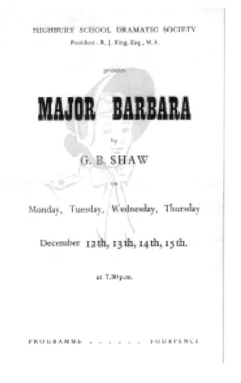

RAF type; "Taffy," who is led into the most outrageous escapades by Porter, and lastly the level headed Mark, who sympathises – and finally falls in love - with Bella.

These parts were realised by Tony Sandell, Alan Watson, John Field, Joseph Glasberg and George Rockingham, who was outstandingly convincing, doing everything "RAF-types" do with great gusto.

Porter's adroitness in running a black market in silk lingerie endears him to Thelma, the flirtatious maid, played by Robin Pearce. Welshman Taffy, the social reformer is disgusted at Porter's activities, although the billetees generally benefit by them.

The play was kept on an even keel by the hilarity of the nocturnal escapades, in contrast to the emotional scenes between Mark and Bella.

Mark Jenkins, playing the frustrated and insignificant Mr. Bounty, who eventually breaks the rule of his wife and comes into his own, must not be forgotten.

Years of experience have set a high standard for performance, scenery &c., which was ably maintained by all concerned in this production.

## *Major Barbara, 1955*

Last year's presentation by the Dramatic Society of George Bernard Shaw's *Major Barbara* – wrote Anthony J. Thorncroft in the January 1956 edition of *The Highburian* Magazine – maintained the tradition of producing alternately humorous and thought-provoking plays. The play is poles apart from the farce, *Worm's Eye View* of 1954. The name of Bernard Shaw strikes terror into everybody under the age of 16, and a good many older. As the cinema world would say, he is not good "box-office". *Major Barbara* is no exception to the general trend of Shaw's work, and the sustained applause at the end of the play spoke much for the quality of the acting by the cast. It was indeed the most agreeable I have seen, making it rather difficult to pick out any stars.

To my mind Robert Thomas stole the limelight in the role of Undershall. Although suffering from a chill, he gave a brilliant performance, commanding the stage in the most difficult role of the play. David Barratt as Major Barbara was also excellent, acting with much more confidence than he did last year.

I am compelled to mention the entire cast, from Harkman and Morecroft, (everyone's idea of a butler) upwards. The weaker sex were admirably portrayed by Patrick Smith, Croggan, Rolfe, and Shepherd, who were not at all prevented from giving fine performances in the other feminine roles by their novel attire. Once again Burt presented his usual inimitable caricature.

In the role of Major Barbara's fiancé and soul-torn student of Greek, Andrew Vrahimedes was very successful, as was Robert Pearce in the role of a society

*Seven of the main characters in G.B.Shaw's "Major Barbara" – back: Harold Burt, David Barrett and Bob Thomas; front: Patrick Smith, Keith Croggon, John Shepherd and John Field.*

beau. John Field and Philip Morgan showed themselves clever actors in the well-portrayed parts of the down-and-outs. Eddy Field gained a round of applause every night for his wholly convincing role as a thug.

Mr. Wood ably supported by Messrs. Beverton and Ward, showed us that he is as able in producing the best-ever acting, as Mr. Leech, his renowned predecessor.

The acting is only half the play however; the other half is the play itself. Does Shaw also deserve a bouquet? I think he does. He is essentially a playwright for older theatre goers, but the Highbury School Dramatic Society's handling of the piece allowed him to make his punches felt, and impressed a relatively youthful audience. If he impressed the young, he surely delighted and provoked the thoughts of the older and more serious of us.

Thanks must go to David Perman *(on leave from National Service in the Army at Aldershot)* for deputising for Thomas so successfully at short notice in the Thursday matinee.

## Chapter Thirteen
# Rambling Reminiscences of the Fifties

## 1.– Desperate Dan & Cow Pie
### by Geoff Jones

To caricature him I would ask you to go to that old copy of *The Beano*, you've got tucked away in the loft, and find the cartoon strip showing "Desperate Dan" scoffing his Cow Pie. That would give you his physical traits, but I doubt if even this very singular fellow would have tempted the wrath of the headmaster by turning up to morning assembly in cowboy gear.

E. G. Taylor, or the Reverend E. G. Taylor, to give him his proper title, for he was the Religious Instruction teacher (or RI, for short) for the whole school. In his lapel he wore the emblem of "The Old Contemptibles," denoting that he had served with the British Expeditionary Force in France at the start of WWI. He was a colossus of a man, and was unique in the culture of the school. He presided over his domain in his study, tucked away in the basement, its walls lined with obscure tomes, which overflowed the shelves, in piles all round the room. If you happened to belong to the school choir, as I did, one had frequent access there. For after every school concert at Easter and Christmas, the whole choir was invited into the great man's den, there to indulge in great platefuls of jelly and blancmange; a welcome reward for having sung oneself hoarse.

He ran the school summer camp at Seaton in Devon which I'm afraid I never attended. The closest I came, was to the adjacent field where, one particular year, to my great surprise, my Boys Brigade Company had decided to encamp for the fortnight. There was a bit of chatter over the hedge/ditch of course; though I don't know how the school camp was run, I do remember that several of the school lads stood wide-eyed at the military-style inspections of boxed blankets, kit layouts, and tightly rolled tent brailing, which happened daily on our side.

A further privilege which being part of the school choir brought was awarded by that other great Christian gentleman of the school, the head himself, Mr. R.J. Marsh, who was also a member. Each term, in recognition of after hours time we gave up to practice, we were allowed an extra half day's holiday.

Apart from the concerts, there was a School Church Service held at Christ Church, Highbury Barn once a term. I remember the first occasion on which I went. The church was quite High, I believe. I had been brought up as a staunch Methodist, with its very simple methods of worship. To be there all dressed up in a cassock, seeing priests wearing brightly coloured robes, the Cross being paraded, made me feel quite uncomfortable. I turned to the boy beside me and asked "this isn't a Catholic Church, is it?" His weak reply, "I don't think so," left me still quite worried about what my God would do, if he found out I'd been taking part in some awful religious burlesque. We had some good solid prejudices in those days.

I didn't often end up for admonishment in the head's office, but I did on one occasion. I never became a prefect, so failed to gain a full appreciation of their duties, but it seemed to us in the lower echelons that they had mainly to do with matters sartorial or janitorial. Anyway, one day I must have stuck my cap in my satchel, or wandered out at lunchtime without a pass, and ended up with prefects' detention after school which I promptly failed to attend.

"I'm sorry, I just honestly forgot to go," I said to the Head. "And I accept your explanation, that you genuinely forgot," he replied, "but it would seem helpful of me to offer you a little *aide-memoire* to ensure it doesn't happen again. Now Jones, we spend time together [the choir] outside of this office, I hope that after what I am about to do, we will still remain friends when you come to leave. Bend over!" After three strikes I thought I was out, and started to lift my head, but another stroke came, and six looked to be on the cards. Mercifully it stopped there at four. Of course, deep down it didn't really hurt a bit, and I love his memory.

Other extra-curricular musical activities included pianoforte lessons. A dozen of us young would-be Paderewskis used to gather in a classroom with one upright piano – 12 silent fingering practice claviers, and the conductor of the then Modern Symphony Orchestra. He sat at a desk manually scoring for a full orchestra, but could be relied on to bellow out, with extreme accuracy, and without seeming loss of concentration from his task "Come on now that's a B flat! No, give me F sharp!" whenever the unlucky one sitting at the "live" instrument misplaced a digit. "Oh go away, and practice it for next week. Next one please!"

Despite this, around the end of the fourth year my prowess in the field lead to me being coerced into playing in a concert arranged by the then Music teacher, Mrs. Gauld. My very halting rendition of the "Fairy Dell Waltz" received few accolades. However, I was filled with amazement by another act by a fellow, I think called Jennings. He formed a cone from newspaper, into which he poured a pint-and-a-half of milk, without spilling a drop. He then unrolled the newspaper, from which the milk had disappeared! Marvellous stuff; and this was half a century before Harry Potter!

Mr. Rosenthal, a refugee from Czechoslovakia, taught us the most perfect French, I'm sure. However when he became excited his English diction became somewhat less than clear, and his mixed metaphors became legend. Made angry by one pupil, who left himself wide open, the master shouted heatedly, " If ze cap fits upon ze shoes, vare zem!" We wondered what the prefects, who monitored compliance with the correct wearing of school uniform at the gates, would have had to say about this unsuitable treatment of a school-cap! This miscreant was luckier than most, however. Mr. Rosenthal had devised a most excruciating means, by which to punish and humiliate those of his pupils who became too cheeky. He would stand close to the offender, many of whom were taller than himself, and take the short hairs of their side-burn between his thumb and index-finger. He would then simply raise his hand, lifting his hapless prey to their feet, and even to their tiptoes, if he were severely displeased with them! Not even the toughest youngster could withstand this approach. It was most effective, and left no marks!

"Charlie" Garrett, whose real Christian name was Edmund, taught History. He was distinguished by his cauliflower ears, which popular rumour ascribed to his having gained a Blue boxing for Oxford. Former staff-room members assert that this affliction was simply a birthmark. He too wore in his lapel the emblem of the Old Contemptibles, as the survivors of the British Expeditionary Force (BEF) in WWI dubbed themselves. They took the name in mocking reference to a speech made by the German Kaiser, who referred to the BEF as "this contemptible little army!" They were the first troops to be sent to France

*This photo shows myself (George Leach), Anthony Thomas who died in 1987, and Kenny Lee – the photographer was Eric Gordon Jones("Jonah"). It was taken outside the art/woodwork rooms. In the background is the British Restaurant, where several of us dined rather than face school dinners – until someone saw a large rat run along the wall and into the restaurant!*

*Fifth Form 1, 1952-53, with Mr. Gillespie – Back row: George Ryb, J. Pilcher, Anthony Thomas, Kenny Lee, Maurice Perlmutter, Robin Lancaster, Spike Gillespie, E.A. Papandreos, Leonard Lippiatt, Albert Spiller and E.R. Davis. Middle row: Sam Levy, Micky Holbrook, Alex "Runki" Roffey, Malcolm Cox, George Snooks and Ken Clark. Front row: M. Williams, Ray Millett, Gilbert Wells, Eric Gordon Jones, Alan Webb and Ray Armitage.*

in 1914, and thousands of them were killed in the opening battles of the campaign on the Somme.

He was rarely seen without his cutdown billiard cue. He never actually used it as an instrument of physical abuse, of course. The tacit threat was always there, however. When he crashed it down on your desk, because of your inattention, you knew it could guarantee one hundred laborious lines. A "But, Sir!" in protest, meant your weekend was definitely going to be ruined, as he swung round casually, redirecting the stick towards the blackboard, on which were inscribed the "five political ambitions of Bismarck'. He would then say, very quietly "Make that two hundred!" He used the next uplift only once to my recollection. I believe it was straight up to five hundred lines.

## 2.– Lulu, Spike and others
### by George Leach

I mostly remember Dennis Lewis's classes, not for the maths, but for the lectures on the rules of football. He was a referee, first class I believe, and a couple of the boys were excellent footballers, Micky Holbrook and Bowie

Young. They would conspire to ask him a question about the rules of the game, and maths would go out of the window for forty minutes or so.

Leslie "Spike" Gillespie was a Canadian, a no-nonsense tough nut, who was a great favourite with us boys. Sometimes in our last year he told us that he intended to leave and write a book. I am almost certain that he said that the title was to be "The Man Who Never Was". I know a book and a film of that name came out a few years later, but I do not know if he had any connection with it or if my memory has played a trick on me.

The Revd. Taylor had an enormous influence on me, even though I had, and have, no religion. He awakened in me a great interest in ancient civilisations and an understanding of the beliefs of other religions, especially Judaism. Also his descriptions of his service in the First World War, in which he was a stretcher-bearer, brought home the full horrors of warfare. I think he was a man who in conscience could not kill, but served with the bravest of the brave.

"Dan" Duffield was, I think, a native of Cumberland and had come into teaching after war service as a sort of apprentice teacher. He did not finally qualify until about our third year, when his fate depended on our test results. For reasons I won't go into, we all did extremely well that year. "Dan" was very popular and of course got his name from Dandruff – does such a thing exist today? He himself saw that only popular teachers had nice names.

Bill Laurie was another popular master, if dangerous to know. We very early learned not to be alone with him. Perhaps in a more tolerant age he would have been less predatory, I don't know. I think he got the sack after I left, and possibly his future would have been bleak. He certainly had more than one bottle of ink spilt on him in the stock room, but of course no one ever complained about him. I think that, as with the Mafia, *omerta* was the rule at that time.

Mr. Davies, Geography, had taught and probably trained in Pontypool and elsewhere in this valley *(George was writing from Cwmbrân in the Eastern valley of Gwent)*. He often spoke feelingly of the terrible poverty that people suffered here. "You boys would not believe it," he would say. As my mother's family had lived here for many generations and had been driven out almost *en masse* by poverty, I could and did believe it.

## 3.– 3B circa 1950
### by John Sanderson

During one fine summer's morning at break time, our class leading light in the English Language and Literature disciplines was busily engaged in his favourite pastime, i.e. reading a tome by one of America's leading and brilliant renowned authors (limited edition). Whilst fervently engrossed in enjoying the profound and meaningful words of America's three times winner of the prestigious Booker Prize, to whit Hank Janson, he was chanced upon by our very own form master, Mr. Leech. Now Mr. Leech, naturally being well disposed to the English Language, was overcome with delight at his star pupil's brilliant choice of reading material and elected to borrow the same. The purpose of this student/teacher exchange was to allow the rest of our class to share in the enjoyment of Hank Janson's erudite and unsurpassed literary skills and vision!

This was achieved by passing the volume to a little known master at Highbury County, who went by the name of Mr. Lincoln (amongst others). Now apart from Latin, his other speciality was "clause analysis" which, incidentally, has now disappeared from the school curriculum. So, one never to be forgotten day, Mr. Lincoln breezed (or flapped) into our classroom, armed with the said book and his customary 12-gauge sawn-off billiard cue. He then sardonically read several paragraphs from H.J.'s novel, culminating with the unforgettable words:

"Don't keep flashing your gossamer-clad knees at me, Tallulah; just keep talking, Sister!"

Upon hearing this, the whole class collapsed with laughter, only to be greeted with Lincoln's never to be forgotten response – "You won't think it's so funny when you have to analyse it!" Silence rained (and I mean rained).

## 4. Reflexive verbs and White Projectiles

If the above appears to register no connection with the reader, please bear with me while I explain.

During my sojourn at Highbury County, I had the pleasure of being taught French by the illustrious bilingual person: Monsieur Cobby. Now in my formative years at H.C. I and my class were totally unaware that George was a comparative "Rookie" compared with other Masters. However, what we were aware of was that, although he was a superb French teacher, his attributes stretched to other directions, i.e. Chemistry. His use of "opaque soft white earthy limestone" had to be seen to be believed. For example:

Mr. Cobby: "Sanderson, how many more times must I tell you. Reflexive verbs take *être!*" This was closely followed by the above mentioned chalk, thrown at Mach 3 speed (no chance to duck) arriving on the side of yours truly's head with unerring accuracy and skill. As far as I can recollect, no miscreant ever had cause to visit the sick room.

Incidentally, most people's memories regarding their first remembered French words are either *Je t'aime* or *Je suis*. Mine happens to be *Le Corrigé*.

## Chapter Fourteen
# *Rambling Recollections of the Sixties*

## *1. Memories of Eddie Hall & Friends*

The next few pages contain not only some recollections of my own, but also those of my contemporaries during those dark days, relived nowadays with varying degrees of hilarity and regret during our occasional drinking sessions at *The White Swan* in Upper Street, Islington. It is noteworthy that many of us, now parents ourselves, have difficulty persuading our incredulous offspring that these stories are true. They may have been embellished with age and in the retelling, but they are nevertheless true!

Despite the appalling institutionalised thuggery allowed by the law in those days, my five years at Highbury eventually provided me with five real O – levels with which to face the real world. Mr. Stanley ("The Martian") Wood had confidently predicted that I would fail to obtain any, but unfortunately I never had the opportunity to tell him how wrong he was! At that time a minimum of two O Levels would virtually guarantee that you would find some sort of job to bring in the pennies, so getting five was a big advantage. I would also have enjoyed showing him the Part 1 Banking Diploma, which I obtained a few years later. Mr. Wood, nicknamed by the boys "The Martian," or "The Mekon" in earlier years, was so called because of the shape of his head; broad at the brow, and narrowing at the chin, seeming disproportionately large for his body.

In World Refugee Year (1960), Mr. King set the school a target of £200 which it far exceeded, collecting £1,100. One of the school's big fund raising successes was the Oxfam Charity Show, in which we all dressed up and played the roles of the pop-idols of the time. Especially memorable bits were:
– Mick White's Jagger impersonation in carpet slippers; this was totally inspired, and we all thought he was so quiet!
– Chris Pichon's Cilla Black impersonation, complete with removable "implants" – (tennis balls actually!)

**Colin Stewart** remembers it like this:
Mr. "Jet" Harris organised the famous Oxfam Charity Concert some time during 1963 (I think), and I was Johnny Kidd! At least I was for about ten seconds!
My band, "The Pirates," – featuring John Quarterman on lead guitar, Tony

Simpson on bass, Ray (Joe) Tozer on rhythm guitar and (I think) Dave Mason on drums – appeared on stage miming the opening of "Shakin' All Over."

'Johnny" came swaggering on stage, wearing his older brother's leather jacket and riding boots, which being several sizes too large, immediately caused him to trip over the microphone lead, and go sprawling on stage, with his black eye-patch firmly planted on the end of his nose. I fear that the applause and mocking cheers were not delivered in recognition of our musical prowess!

**Bill Champney** recalls: I took part in the Charity concert; I was the drummer in "The Kinks!" Nobody could have been less like their drummer than I was! Fat and short sighted, (so I have not really changed!) and as I did not have a red jacket, I turned one which had a hideous gold lining inside out!

I recall Bob Bedell impersonating Tom Jones, wearing a pair of Army boots. Two Sixth formers, Malcolm Phillips, and another, (whose name I just cannot recall) were impersonating the Righteous Brothers.

When R. J. King retired from the Headship in 1965, Mr. Stanley Wood took over as Acting Head. He had the irritating mannerism of holding his hand up to his face, in the attempt to mask the fact that he was using his thumb to pick his nose!

In Morning Assembly form 1H stood in the front of the stage, by the steps. One morning I noticed "The Martian" tear his trousers on a projecting nail. He still wore that patched suit, when he became Acting Head five years later.

One Fourth year class produced a mock *This Is Your Life*, with a file containing many anecdotes about "The Martian," and a caricature, made up from a comic-book picture of an alien's head mounted on a drawing of his lanky body below.

Highbury County was probably one of the few schools in London with an indoor swimming pool. Although many would think that we were fortunate, for it seems that most of us were capable of paddling at least a few strokes before we left, the pool itself left much to be desired. The pool was filled twice a week. So the water was crystal clear for the first period on Monday morning, but by Wednesday morning it resembled nothing so much as dark green slimy bath water!

Our first-year PE and swimming teacher, to whom we shall refer as 'G,' appeared to us eleven-year-olds as though he should have retired several years earlier. He would amuse himself by exhorting us to "Get those backs dry!" while peering over the cubicle doors.

**Richard Dawes** takes up the story:

In 1H the first swimming lesson was the selection of the "schwimmahs." The "non-schwimmahs" walked around the side to form a group at the shallow end, while the "schwimmahs" proved their ability by doing a length. Surprisingly, some boys who completed a length were still classed as "non-schwimmahs." I was very irked by this, and after a couple of lessons I slipped back into the "schwimmahs" group. I remember some classmates' looks of astonishment when I got away with this piece of sheer cheek!

**Eddie Hall** resumes:

Every new term G had a ritual selection of the Gym Teams. Firstly captains would be selected, who then took turns to choose their teams. One summer term, about a third of our class conspired to take advantage of G's very poor memory for names by nominating Mick Ferriter, who was very unfit, for captain of a team. When Mick's name was called, G responded "Eckshellant choishe," and beckoned Mick up to the front. In the moment G recognised the nominee, he turned bright red and was speechless for several seconds, before asking Mick to return to his place on the bench with obvious embarrassment. G now turned on Ned Clayton, who had made the actual nomination, and just about managed to splutter, in his best Colonel Blimp style: "You are a Cad, schir, an absholute cad! Leave my gymnashium thish minute!

By this time most of us were doubled up with laughter, and G became even more cross, as he realised that he had been the victim of a conspiracy. Completely overwhelmed by events, he could only manage to wag his crooked finger at us in admonition.

**Colin Stewart** recounts his recollections of G in PT and Games sessions:

As he saw it, G's chief role at Highbury County was as "Head of Physical Education". The one thing that could frustrate him above all other was the weather. Gales at lunchtime or heavy thunderstorms meant waterlogged pitches at Highams Park, and no prospect of games being playable. In the event of snow and ice covering North London, swimming in the unheated pool at Highbury would have to be called off as fit only for masochists or the insane.

Imagine then the scene: Mr. Liddamore's French lesson, just before lunch. Enter G, creeping through the doorway like a shorter latter-day version of Uriah Heep. He sidles up to the bored-looking French master, and whispers: "'Scuse me, Mr. L., I'm sorry to interrupt you, but do you think I might have a quick word with the boys, only a couple of seconds?" L. gestures assent.

Suddenly becoming stern and erect, G faces the class and announces severely, "GAMES ARE ORF! GAMES ARE ORF!" With his smile returning, he now says, "Thank you very much Mr. L. I'm sorry to have troubled you."

With swimming however, the agony would be prolonged until the actual hour arrived. We would sit there in class, awaiting G's announcement. He would creep into the classroom, rubbing his hands together, and in a friendly and conspiratorial voice, would tell us, "Brrr! It's a bit cold in the pool today boys. I think I shall have to make it a voluntary swimming session." Then more sternly, "All those wishing to schwim, follow me!" Finally he would add, with his usual sneer, "The babies can stay behind!"

**Len Ladd** commented: Remember G's total amazement and disbelief when anyone complained that the pool was too cold!

Once we had been "de-loused" by immersion in the cold shower, we were again divided into "schwimmahs" and "non-schwimmahs." The "non-schwimmahs" huddled together at the shallow end, under the watchful gaze of G, who was armed as ever with his famous "long-handled mop."

We were all given white plastic floats, on to which we were instructed to cling as we lined up on one side of the pool. G would then give the order, "One width of the bath, – dog-paddle – GO!" Utter pandemonium then ensued, with legs and arms flying about all over the place. Floats and their owners became separated, and if any poor sod dared to reach for the safety of the side of the pool, G would firmly beat them off with his sodden "long-handled" mop, shouting at them to "GET BACK!"

My most enduring memory of G however, is the picture of him on Sports Day at Parliament Hill Fields. There he stood at the starting line, smartly clad in blazer and white flannels, with a "cheesecutter" cap. He then raised his starting pistol, bent his legs, and clutching his thigh with his free hand, screamed, "Marks, ... Set!" Then came a loud "Crack!" from the pistol; he leapt to attention and marched off with his chest puffed out, totally oblivious to the complete chaos which he had just created. Sometimes people ask how I can remember, — I wonder how anyone could ever forget him!

**Colin Stuart** tells us, G also taught Maths. I recall that on my first day at Highbury County, several of the second year boys in the playground warned us to "Beware of G!" During the early '60s G. was Head of Physical Education and the School Tailor, as well as being a Steward at Arsenal Football Club. He also instructed first year pupils in the art of handwriting and the basic skills of Maths. His strange antics and derisive manner left a lasting impression on many of us. Even forty years later, when two or more of us get together for the odd pint or two, his at times bizarre behaviour remains the subject of much mirth and frivolity.

With the help of Ken Tipple, I have recalled some of the more bizarre moments. Should anyone who did not attend Highbury County School come to read this, I must assure them none of the following is a figment of our imaginations!

"It was our first day at Highbury, and were are awaiting the appearance of the teacher who was to instruct us in the art of handwriting. A short, bald, erect and red-necked character, carrying some books under his arm came into the classroom. He placed the books on the desk in absolute silence, turned to the blackboard, and wrote in large precise letters: G * * *.”

He turned to regard the class of nervous looking eleven-year-olds through his metal rimmed spectacles, and wrinkled his nose as though there were a bad smell emitting from somewhere. He said: “ My name is G.” If you play ball with me, then I will play ball with you; but if any boy steps out of line, I will come down on him like a ton of bricks!”

He then began to issue out the exercise books, instructing us to enter our names on the front label, together with the legend, “WRITING BOOK.” He walked between the rows of desks inspecting the results until he found what he had been looking for. He ordered his victim to stand up, and with a look of utter amazement on his face, announced: “There’s a fellah here who can’t spell ‘writing’. Well, I don’t know! Whatever will your dear old mother think? &c., &c.”

We were all then ordered to put our pens on our desks, and he started to inspect them, paying particular attention to the nibs.

“What’s that?” he asked some poor unsuspecting lad with a fine-nib fountain pen.

“It’s a Parker pen, Sir. My father bought it for my birthday.”

“Don’t mind me giving you a bit of advice, do you?” G replied. “Throw it under a bus! Then go to the School secretary – Mrs. C. – and give her my compliments. Ask her for a School pen & nib.”

Len Westoby similarly recalls G inspecting a Parker fountain pen, owned by another class member.

“Well boy, you might use it for digging potatoes, but it won’t do for writing!”

Having been instructed in the correct formation of every letter in the alphabet, we were instructed to begin copying from Charles Dickens’s *A Christmas Carol*. He inspects the results, then announced his Number One rule in writing: “ALL ONE WAY.’

“I don’t care if your writing slopes backwards, forwards or upright, as long as it goes ALL ONE WAY!”

Mine unfortunately, did not go all one way! In fact it went several different ways, and still does to this day. This meant that my mark fell below the accepted level, and I was ordered to attend the “Half past eight Class,”

“Report to me at half past eight on Monday morning, please, and attend every day until your writing improves.”

So there we would stand at half past eight every morning – boys from different classes – in a line with our school caps planted firmly on our heads, until the famous "Austin of England" poodled up to the main gate. He would then carry his cricket bag past the line of boys, who would all have to touch their caps and say "Good morning, Sir!" His demeanour and the tone of voice in his reply would clearly indicate the level of achievement he would expect from us on that particular day.

G took his role as teacher of Mathematics to the first year boys very seriously indeed. On days when he was teaching Maths, he would exchange his usual garb of cricket flannels, Gabardine raincoat, flat cap and suede shoes for a grey suit, worn with a regimental tie and brown brogue shoes.

Through each new term's tuition his mentor and guide was his textbook, *First Year Mathematics* by H.E. Parr. He would choose the two biggest lads in the form, Ian Sams and Tony Simpson, (who just happened to sit next to each other).

"You, Primrose, hand out these textbooks to the boys on my left, and you, Matilda, hand these books out to the boys on my right. The only times when G ever smiled were when he was taking the mickey – usually by giving someone a derisory nickname; Ken Tipple became "Triple," John Quarterman became "Truant." (This may have had something to do with the latter one-day deciding to quit school to walk the streets of Islington.)

The rest of us took it in turn to share the epithet, "The Form Dunce." Chapter One in H.E. Parr's textbook describes the mathematical formulae for three-dimensional shapes. This prompted G in his choice of subject for the new boys' first homework.

"Go home and construct a cube and a cuboid from some suitable material," he instructed. The following day we had to display the results of our endeavours for his inspection. There was an assortment of exhibits made from cereal packets, shoeboxes, greeting cards &c. As he was surveying this miscellany, many of which were falling to pieces, his usually florid face grew even more roseate in hue. He finally exploded when Cliff Headley produced a sad looking cube, which he had carefully produced from several editions of the *Islington Gazette*.

"Whatsh thish?" he cried, "lasht nightsh fish and chipsh?" His strange manner of speech, as if he had his mouth full of cotton wool, always became more pronounced when he became angry.

While he sat marking homework, and we were working out exercises from "Parr," the restlessness would set in. Tozer catapulted a paper pellet in the direction of Stoney's ear with a ruler. Tipple turned round doing Quasimodo impressions at the giggling Yates, while Mason offered Wagner a penny for three blackjacks. Without even glancing up, G would murmur, "Mumbling!" The resulting silence would not last long. Five minutes later, this time in utter amazement, G would bark: "There'sh shtill shomebody mumbling, WHY?"

Finally his voice would become almost a scream, "There'sh shtill a wretched fellah mumbling! If I find 'im, I'll come down on 'im like a ton of bricksh!"

Here is another gem from one of G's Maths lessons:

"Apples are thruppence; pears are tuppence. "Triple', if I give you two apples, would you give me four pears? Quickly, boy!"

"Yes, Sir!" replied Ken Tipple.

"Well I don't know!" said "G," "Stuart, you're not the Form Dunce any more, "Triple" is! Hit him, Matilda! Hit him hard!"

John Quarterman once asked if anyone could elaborate on G's "Congruent Triangles." Well, John here goes:

"Two shides, one angle, trianglesh are congruent. Two anglesh, one shide; trianglesh are shimilarly congruent!"

There was the famous occasion when G had discovered that three of the pupils had forged their homework marks. He walked solemnly into the room. His grey suit had been exchanged for a black one, with a handkerchief in the breast pocket, and a white shirt. He sat at his desk and composed himself for a minute, took off his glasses, and began polishing them carefully with the handkerchief. Replacing them, he rose slowly, and in a voice trembling more with sorrow than anger, he announced conspiratorially,

"Boys, we have criminals in the form!"

Then he raised his voice: "Shtand up, the criminalsh!"

A silence ensued.

"I shaid shtand up the criminalsh!"

"Who, me, sir?" whispered a shaky voice.

*"Yesh,* you *shir!* You know who I mean!"

The three lads were packed off to the Headmaster's study.

"Give the Headmaster my complimentsh, and tell 'im you are the criminalsh!"

Normality resumed, and the homework for the following night was given out: "H.E. Parr, page 5, questions 1 to 12; page 8, questions 4 and 5."

Peering cheerfully over his glasses, he added, "That'sh all!"

**Richard Dawes** recounts another tale:

Some will recall that the classroom windows had wide sills, which extended a long way either side of the window frame. One day several pupils were amused to see "T" cleaning a white mess off the roof of his car, parked in the drive below, to reveal a large dent. This was the unforeseen result of some jolly classroom jape, to which David Greene was an innocent witness.

Every day, one boy had yoghurt, which came in glass jars in those days. Somebody took it from his bag and hid it around the corner of the windowsill.

When the owner could not find his yoghurt, he took the prime suspect's bag, and hid it around the same corner of the windowsill, dislodging the yoghurt jar to fall upon the roof of the car beneath.

(**Brian Boyle** *commented: this prompts the recollection of a similar incident during the summer term of 1955, when my first year sixth form group occupied a common room on the top floor overlooking the south playground. A sixth form privilege was to take our daily third-of-a-pint milk ration back to our room. Too lazy to return the bottles to the hall downstairs, we began to stockpile the empties on the wide window ledge outside. Unfortunately, while Percy Clavey, the Schoolkeeper, was standing in the playground below one day, a strong gust of wind dislodged a number of the bottles, narrowly missing the poor man, to shatter on the Tarmac around him. Fortunately, there was no conclusive proof of our guilt, so we were severely reminded that milk bottles should be returned to the hall when consumed.*)

All these reminiscences of crimes lead on naturally to consider punishments, just and unjust. **Bill Champney** has good reason to remember "Taffy" and his plastic truncheon – because Bill thought it would make a welcome change from the slipper, and gave it to him! But the wily "Taffy" filled it with paper, making it the ultimate deterrent. He also had a fondness for Bass bitter ale, and an aversion to watery beer!

According to **Lennie Ladd**, one or other of the PE teachers had a selection of plimsolls and canes in a cupboard. Offenders (or victims) were invited to choose the method of their own punishment. Whichever version was chosen he recalls, "they both b****y hurt!"

**Mike Lewis, Chris Pichon** and **Len Westoby** corroborate each other's testimony in remembering Mr. King's predilection for using progressive degrees of punishment. First offenders might get away with a scrub from his coarse stubble of his chin; a further offence brought a few strokes of the slipper, while recidivists could look forward to the cane. Mike recalls that when Mr. King considered the dinner queue to be making too much noise one afternoon, he used the slipper on all 20 or 30 boys in the queue.

**Eddie Hall** has strong recollection of the public caning.

One afternoon, he says, the whole school were summoned to an assembly in the school hall. Such an assembly was hitherto unheard of, so there was an atmosphere of extreme trepidation in the hall – and with good cause.

It was alleged that three pupils had been caught stealing while away on a school trip. One after the other, the three were led up on to the stage, where they were made to face the rear of the stage (i.e. backs to the assembly), drop their trousers and bend over. The supposed ringleader received six strokes, while the other two received three strokes each.

**Richard Dawes, Mike Lewis** and **Colin Stuart** have put together their recollections of one of the more colourful characters on the staff in those days.

Our Chemistry teacher was a real "nutty professor" type, nicknamed "Polly" because of his prominent nose, who could not control a class. He it was who one day uttered the classic gaffe: "Every time I open my mouth, some fool speaks!"

During one lesson when we were completely out of control, Polly mistakenly appealed to our supposedly sympathetic natures, by divulging that his son was seriously ill and in an oxygen tent in hospital. At which DM commented "He cannot be too bad if he's gone camping!" It seemed very funny at the time.

Polly was demonstrating how to make Sulphur Dioxide in the laboratory, by heating copper metal with sulphuric acid, and manganese dioxide as the catalyst. The chemical formulae and the reaction equation were drawn on the blackboard, and the equipment was assembled on his bench. Polly lit the gas burner and the class waited… and waited, … and still waited.

When no reaction had taken place after ten minutes, Polly added more copper, but as there was still no reaction, he added more acid. He repeatedly added more of each ingredient, until the flask was almost full, but to no avail. Then suddenly the reaction began, but instead of a gentle bubbling, a great foaming reaction took place, and clouds of poisonous gas were filling the room. We were forced to retreat into the playground. One lad was sent home because the gas triggered an asthma attack. Presumably K., the Headmaster would have held some kind of inquest on this near disaster, but we heard no more of the incident.

## 2. Polly's Fireworks

As recounted by **Ken (Ben) Tipple**

In the following tale of the chemical Laboratory antics of Polly and his Middle-eastern Laboratory Assistant, Achmet some events which took place on different occasions have been juxtaposed for the sake of brevity and effect. In all other respects however, this is a true story.

To begin the lesson Polly would produce his stick of white chalk from his jacket pocket and commence to explain the theory of the experiment, which he was about to perform, by writing the complicated formulae on the revolving blackboard. On the reverse side of this revolving board usually were written the highly complex and advanced formulae, which Polly had prepared as the subject for a subsequent sixth form lecture later that day.

Dave Mason contrived to distract Polly's attention while Lennie Ladd disappeared behind the board and proceeded to erase these carefully prepared formulae. When he was discovered, Ladd was dismissed from the laboratory amid uproar, at which Polly exploded with "Get out Stubbs!"

Now whenever our behaviour had caused his displeasure, Polly would make us sit and read in silence, the Chemistry textbook, of which "Stubbs" was the author. Now as the first three letters of the author's name and of my own name – Stuart – were the same, I had been nicknamed "Stubbs."

As soon as Polly shouted, "Get out Stubbs!" I would get up and start to walk towards the door, only to be roughly manhandled back to my place by the now fuming Polly.

Once we had settled down, Polly became mollified, and the experiment would recommence. Hydrogen was to be produced by electrolysis with water (or something like that), Everyone was ordered to the back of the laboratory; having placed everything within reach, Achmet too would retreat. Polly, holding a taper shakily over the test-tube cried out "Get Down!" At this, even with our hands over our ears, we could clearly hear a dull "Phut" emitted from the test tube, which was greeted by further uproar. Dave Mason called out, "Where's the mushroom cloud?"

As the lesson drew to a close, Polly looked at his watch, and cried, "Bunsen's out!" This was the cue for everyone to throw the iron filings, which they had previously concealed about themselves, into the Bunsen burners, and to sing out: "Light up the sky with "Polly's Fireworks!" while Geoff Yates let out a cry of "Wheeee!" The lesson dissolved into utter chaos!

**Bill Szelazek** recalls the most disliked staff member of their era. When G retired in about 1964 a new PE teacher, whom we shall call "HJH," was appointed. He was ex-RAF, and a bully whose physical prowess did not match up to his own imagination of it. He would constantly pick on those of us who were, shall we say, of a less than athletic build or disposition. For those of us who were there in the early 1960s, "HJH" must be a contender for the title of "He who left the most lasting impression."

Unlike "Ben" Tipple, who was one of the best goalkeepers we had, football was never one of my favourite pastimes, and I was only too keen to take the alternative offered by cross-country running over at Hackney Marshes.

The history teacher who used to accompany us, because of his girth, would wait patiently at the changing rooms while we went off around the circuit. I can picture the route now: over the footbridge, turn right and complete one lap, returning over the same footbridge.

But there was a shelter a few hundred yards beyond the footbridge, and after a few weeks we realised that it would be much easier to wait in the shelter for 15 minutes, having a cigarette, instead, before returning – all puffed out from our strenuous exertions. Then one week, as we were enjoying our cigarettes, when who should turn up but "HJH'. He then made us run around the circuit twice, while he strode out with us to make sure nobody dropped out along the way.

**Ian Sams** added: At a swimming gala he told me that I had hit the ropes during a race because my right arm was much stronger than my left. When I argued he became angry as usual, and shouted at me that he was the PE teacher, and my job was to listen and learn. I pointed out that, had he bothered to watch me in any of the other sports in which I had represented the school, he would have noticed that I both bowled and put the shot, left handed. I don't think he ever spoke to me again!

## 3. Memories of Steve Barrett

Steve Barrett from Leigh-on-Sea writes:

I entered the school in the autumn of 1963 and had finished my fourth year when it closed down in 1967. I started in Form 1B with Mr. Mudd, the mathematics teacher as our form master; he later married the lady who taught German in the school.

Mr. Myers, who was a youngish, if rather eccentric chap, taught us Latin. In the first lesson he paced up and down in front of the class with his hands behind his back, while repeating "ambulo," which we were apparently supposed to figure out meant "I walk." A lesson or two later he brought a toy plastic doll into the lesson, and marched its legs back and forth on the desk, saying: "puella ambulat." Entertainment over, we then knuckled down to several years of Latin grammar.

Another particularly memorable character from my early years was Mr. Hirst, the P.E. master. He was undoubtedly the most sadistic teacher I ever encountered, and was the bane of our lives. He was responsible for my never learning to swim. After a single lesson, in which I was dumped into the freezing cold water in the swimming pool, I got a virtually permanent sick note from my GP on the grounds of asthma, and never went into the pool again.

Our English master was Mr. Wood, the Deputy Head, - nicknamed "The Mekon', after the evil extraterrestrial strip cartoon character with a large cranium, who appeared in *The Eagle* comic book.

A somewhat buxom Miss Elliott, who seemed rather to fancy herself, taught us French. In the fourth year the boys became quite cruel to her, and I remember her storming out of the classroom in tears, after she had been pelted with paper aeroplanes as she turned to face the blackboard. She remained with us until the final year of the grammar school, but I believe she then left because of "nervous stress".

At the end of the first year we were reorganised into three forms, and my friend John Stocks and I ended up in a supposedly upper class group, designated as 2G. We were then required to choose whether to continue with Latin, or to switch to learning German. I chose to continue with Latin, because I had already done a year of it. We now had a different teacher for Latin, Mr. Walker, who was overweight and depressive, and apparently agonised over trying to reconcile his devout Christianity with fervent Communism.

He tried to establish a rapport with the boys by throwing the odd small packet of sweets to any boy who correctly answered some obscure point. He ceased doing this after a time, and when the boys asked why, he replied that he had been told "to stop currying favour with the junior boys". Retrospectively, this fits into pattern, since I recall him exposing himself to the boys in the changing room during a games afternoon some years later. It was further reputed that some years later he appeared in court charged with alleged "mischievous doings with young boys". It is believed that he died some years ago.

I remember our fairly gossipy Chemistry master, Mr. Cropley, told us much later that shortly after the grammar school had closed down, and Mr. Rhodes Boyson was Headmaster of the new Comprehensive, Mr. Walker went to see the Headmaster. According to Mr. Cropley, before entering the room Mr. Walker overheard the Headmaster saying to someone else words to the effect of "…a pity about Myers handing in his resignation, shame it isn't Walker!" Apparently Mr. Walker turned away and returned to the staff room to lament the results of his eavesdropping.

After E. G. Taylor came a younger religious teacher called Harrison, whose views tended towards racism. He would occasionally talk about "the Blacks" and "the Pinks." This latter term was a substitution of his own for "Whites," which obviously meant something to him that others could never quite penetrate. I was never in his class but was told that he would ask misbehaving boys to spell the word "Mediterranean." If they got it wrong he would grab them by their scalp hair and give them a "head roll," which was seemingly designed to dislocate the cervical vertebrae.

Another teacher who comes to mind briefly was a Physics teacher whose name was I believe, Mr. Greenberg, who bore a concentration camp number tattooed on his arm ...

*Steve Barrett's recollections are continued in Chapter 17 "Twilight of the Gods"*

## Chapter Fifteen
# *The 1953 Panoramic Photo* *

*\* taken in the new playground on Highbury New Park –
photo courtesy of V.G. Downing.*

## Chapter Sixteen
# *The 1964 Panoramic Photo* *

*\* taken in the south playground on the corner of
Highbury Grove and Highbury New Park*

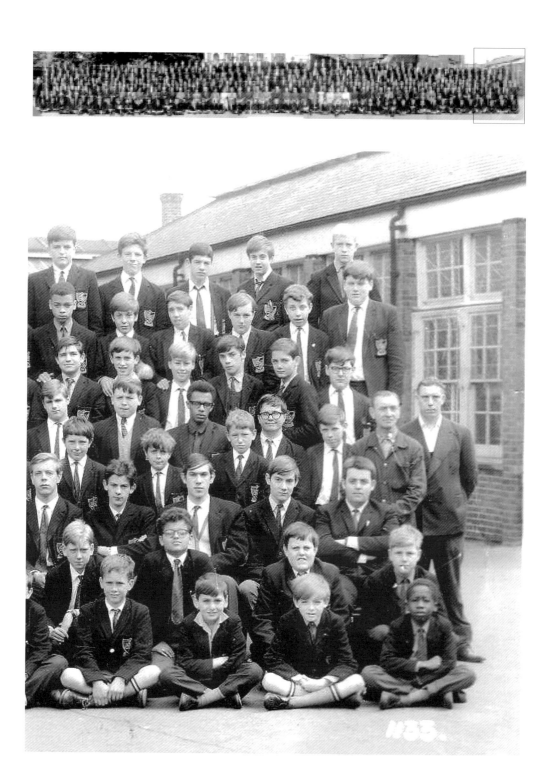

## Chapter Seventeen
# Twilight of the Gods

*And all our yesterdays have lighted fools*
*The way to dusty death. Out, out, brief candle!*
*Life's but a walking shadow, a poor player,*
*That struts and frets his hour upon the stage,*
*And then is heard no more; it is a tale*
*Told by an idiot, full of sound and fury,*
*Signifying nothing.*

Shakespeare, *Macbeth*

All good things must come to an end – so says the old adage. Since 1938 Headmasters Marsh and King, as well as parents and governors had campaigned for a new school to be built; they had persuaded the Education Authority, provisional funding and outline Planning permission had been granted. When the Second World War broke out the scheme was postponed for the duration of hostilities, but not entirely forgotten. Mr. Marsh retired before his dream could be realised.

Mr. King was soon to resume the campaign, while government policy towards "selective" education was changing under pressure from post-war egalitarianism. The stage was being set for the dismantling of the Grammar School system, and Mr. King, unwittingly perhaps, began setting the scenery with his address at the school's Speech Day in 1958. On 28 October of that year, the *Islington Gazette* carried under the heading:

### TRAFFIC NOISE HINDERS SCHOOL LESSONS

*Conditions make Highbury Head*
*"wish for a fire – in evil moments"*

Presenting his annual report at Highbury School Speech Day on Thursday, the Headmaster, Mr. R.J. King commented on the inadequacy of the overcrowded school buildings at Highbury Grove. He told the assembly at Archway Central Hall that it was true that a school was not just a building.

"But there does come a time," he added, "when material conditions affect the spirit and work of everyone. I am sure that the noise of lorries and buses, in what was once a quiet byway, not only affects work but saps mental energy."

"I can only say that when five o'clock comes round I am dead whacked and tired. Sometimes in my evil moments, I wish we could have a fire!"

After the applause, which greeted this remark, had died away, Mr. King pointed out that since 1924 Highbury School had been promised a new building. There was always a reason, but year by year the project had been put off, while wonderful buildings "go up all around us."

Of the school's work in general Mr. King said he was "far better pleased" than he had been the previous year. He did not know the reason for this improvement – but he was delighted to see it. Highbury boys were now attending universities in many parts of the country and the majority of the boys in the present Sixth form – which was the largest ever – would also be going to universities. Turning to the community life of the school, Mr. King commented that the general conduct and appearance of the boys was satisfactory and much improved. He was still a little worried however, about the behaviour of boys who went about in groups.

With the new decade of the '60s, a new school seemed to come very much closer. But what sort of a school would it be: grammar or comprehensive? The final choice of a comprehensive is often blamed on the new Labour government which took power in October 1964 – that was the opinion of many parents and the Conservative party in Islington. But the decision was in effect taken by the Inner London Education Authority (ILEA) set up by the Conservatives as one consequence of their abolition of the LCC. On 19 March 1965, Mr. King himself made this clear in a letter which he had published in the *North London Press*.

"I would like to comment on the new proposals for the future of Highbury and Barnsbury Schools summarised recently in the Press. The original London School Plan of 1947 envisaged a comprehensive school at Highbury; in 1962, the Revised London Plan proposed instead that new buildings should be erected on an enlarged site for both schools, each to retain its identity but sharing important facilities, such as a library, assembly halls and swimming bath, equal to those of any comprehensive school. More important, the two schools agreed to work closely together, especially at sixth form level. This imaginative interpretation of the comprehensive ideal was accepted by the governors, headmasters and staffs of both schools, and the architect produced an exciting group of buildings to express the joint enterprise. Now the ILEA has suddenly dropped the scheme before it has even been tried and reverted to the plan of a single comprehensive school of the normal pattern: so that within a few years Highbury and Barnsbury would both disappear.

"My staff and I feel that political expediency has overcome enlightened educational policy. The 1962 scheme offered a challenge in which senior boys in particular, while remaining leaders in their own school, could opt for whole courses or individual subjects in the other, and activities like orchestra and choir would be combined. At the same time, such endemic problems of a large school as the burden of administration and paper work, and the sheer waste of time in moving classes over a large site, would be avoided."

Mr. King went on to give a dire warning, that the spread of intellectual ability among the intakes of the two schools was very narrow and might be reduced even further in a large comprehensive – and there would be problems of discipline "in an area already notorious for crimes of violence"

The letter was typical of Mr. King, bringing the argument down from the rarefied strata of educational principles to the needs of individual boys. It was intended not only to warn parents and others about the new plan but also, ideally, to influence voting within the ILEA before it came to its final decision. But on 13 April 1965, the *Islington Gazette* reported that the ILEA's Schools and Schools Planning Sub-Committee had confirmed the plan. The full ILEA confirmed the plan in May, but it was still up to the Minister of Education to approve the decision.

Mr. King retired at the end of July 1965 and was succeeded by Mr. Stan Wood as Acting Head. It was in the following autumn term that ILEA's plan for Highbury received central government approval. As the *North London Press* reported on 17 December 1965 under the headline FEWER GRAMMAR PLACES AFTER SCHOOLS MERGER:

> The Minister of Education, Mr. Anthony Crosland has approved the plan to merge Highbury School and Barnsbury School for Boys into a Comprehensive. In making this decision he has rejected Highbury parents' plea that joining the two schools would lower the standards, both in work and behaviour.
>
> A joint letter of protest, condemning the closure of the two schools and their replacement by a comprehensive school, has been sent to the Minister by Mr. John Holderness and Mr. Alan Hardy, the respective prospective Conservative candidates for the East and South west Islington constituencies. They handed the letter to a ministry official on Tuesday afternoon.
>
> Mr. Holderness told the *North London Press*, "We are disgusted at what has happened. The decision to amalgamate the two schools has been forced at every step, despite the protests made by many hundreds of people. We

deplore the throwing aside of a good school for the sake of carrying out a doctrine."

Highbury Grammar School has some 500 pupils and about 900 boys attend Barnsbury Secondary School. Highbury School Parents' Association collected nearly 10,000 signatures for two petitions to the GLC and the Minister of Education. The majority of the parents of Barnsbury School is, however in favour of the comprehensive scheme, and supported a petition signed by more than 6,000 people.

The proposal for a merger into a 1,400 – strong school in 1967 was approved in April by the school's planning subcommittee, and approved by the Inner London Education Authority in May.

Work on the erection of two buildings on a site in Highbury Grove adjacent to Highbury School has already started. At first the buildings were intended for "twin" schools, that is, the two schools would share a main site, but would remain separate. Now they will form a joint comprehensive school.

Despite the protests and petitions, in certain quarters the decision to go for a single comprehensive school was seen as inevitable. Mrs. Mary Pothecary, secretary of Highbury Parents' Association, told the newspaper: "We are naturally disappointed at the Minister's decision, but feel that it was inevitable. The committee is concerned at the Minister's statement that the academic intake will be reduced, but we know that all Highbury parents will co-operate to enable the best results to be obtained for the benefit of their children. We would like to think that, whatever the outcome, the traditions of Highbury will be maintained."

Mr. E.S. Wood, acting Headmaster of Highbury School, said he felt that the decision was inevitable in view of the government's policy on comprehensive schools. He added: "We expected this to happen. What I regret is the fact that the academic intake will be smaller." He regretted much more the sheer numbers, since it would be difficult for one Headmaster to get to know 1,400 pupils. Mr. Wood stressed that the staff of Highbury School accepted the decision and were prepared to co-operate very fully with staff at Barnsbury School.

The scene was now set for the final run-down of Highbury County Grammar School and its replacement by a larger comprehensive to be known as Highbury Grove School. Buildings for the latter were already being constructed on the new playground area, adjacent to Highbury New Park, and when these were completed the old building would be demolished. This programme was set to be completed by the beginning of the autumn term, 1967.

## Going to Pot

Steve Barrett from Leigh-on Sea continues his recollections as a pupil who experienced both regimes at Highbury: "In the Third – and finally and definitively in the Fourth Year – one very much got the impression that the School was going to pot. There seemed to be quite a turnover of teachers. Mr. King had gone, and it was well known that the place was to be pulled down to make way for the Comprehensive. With the limited future of the school, one imagines that recruitment must have been a problem.

"Perhaps it was the age group I was in, but behaviour seemed abysmal. Between lessons people would play football in the classrooms and smash windows. The pupils progressively damaged the fabric of the building and fire extinguishers were let off; there were even instances of air guns being fired along the corridors. The school was going to be demolished and one got the impression that nobody – even the teachers – really cared; the destructive element in the psyche of the children seized the opportunity to "put the boot in".

The *North London Press* on the 19 August 1966 carried a photograph of the construction site in Highbury Grove, published above the following caption:

## Islington's Newest School

Steady progress is being made on the construction of buildings of Islington's new comprehensive school, to be formed by the merger of Highbury School, Highbury Grove, and Barnsbury School for Boys. The School, which is going up on a site adjacent to Highbury School, is expected to be ready for use by September 1967.

It will eventually provide accommodation for about 1,400 boys, including pupils from Laycock Secondary School, which is to be closed. The Headmaster will be Mr. Rhodes Boyson, the present 40 year-old head of Montefiore Comprehensive School, Tower Hamlets.

So that was the end of Highbury County School. Meetings, petitions and protests all went unheeded. Prime Minister Harold Wilson's promise that grammar schools would only be abolished "over my dead body!" was just another sound bite, forgotten as soon as said. Social engineering in education began by dismantling the grammar school system. The views of the people were heard, but dismissed as irrelevant by the politicians, and the merger went ahead, over "Boggy" Marsh's dead body, rather than Harold Wilson's. The merger of the schools provided a stepping stone in the careers of Dr. Rhodes Boyson and his successor, Mr. Laurie Norcross.

*Dr. Rhodes Boyson, first Headmaster of Highbury Grove Comprehensive School – later Conservative MP for Brent, an Education Minister and Sir Rhodes Boyson.*

Let Steve Barrett, who was a pupil at Highbury at the time, have the last words of our story:

"I clearly remember standing in the new school sometime after it opened, watching the cranes demolish the old buildings with large metal balls that were swung into the brickwork. I was then in the Fifth Year of the new comprehensive. A younger boy from one of the other amalgamated schools was standing next to me, and I told him that I could remember the intricacies of the building so well.

"You must feel really sad seeing it knocked down," he said. I said that I wasn't.

"My memories of the place were of being a frightened insignificant child in a stern and unhappy environment. I find it difficult to fit into context those four years I spent at Highbury County School. I had been to a modern and progressive (if pretty useless) primary school in Highbury Quadrant and afterwards was in a 'modern' comprehensive, before going on to a modern University at Southampton. Looking back it's rather as if those four years had catapulted me 60 years back in time. I think that Highbury County was an anachronism when I got there: it was inevitable that time would overtake it."

## Chapter Eighteen
# Old Highburians, Past & Present

Before 1967 the Old Highburians' Association was very much an extension of the school itself. This may seem obvious but it is worth stating now that the school has disappeared, and yet the Old Highburians live on. In fact, like the proverbial Phoenix they have risen from the ashes and not for the first time.

In 1939 *The Highburian Magazine* reported that the Old Boys had "weathered a crisis" and were "forging ahead" (this chapter is bound to have more than its fair share of mixed metaphors!) The first AGM of the year 1938-39 held on the 19 May had been so poorly attended "that the existence of the Association was severely threatened." *Headmaster Gallops to the Rescue*. Mr. Marsh, then at the height of his persuasive powers and no doubt appealing to patriotism "in this hour of crisis" as well as loyalty, sent out an appeal, following which an extraordinary AGM was held at the school on the 16 June, attended by 60 Old Boys and a good number of the staff. This proves, said the magazine, "that in spite of the usual apathy shown to Associations there is a deep underlying sentiment amongst Old Students." Be that as it may, the range of Old Boys' activities reported in the magazine – a successful football season, aided by two fund-raising dances held at the Manor House Tavern, an enthusiastic though not winning cricket section, and the "outstanding event of the season", the Dinner and Dance held at "Ye Mecca", Finsbury Circus – all that was evidence of thriving interest and it could well have been boredom with AGM business which kept so many Old Boys away. Anyway, the OHA survived and during the war did sterling work in keeping Old Highburians in touch with each other and providing a "comfort fund" for those in the forces.

It is not surprising that Mr. Marsh's retirement in 1953 was one of the high points of the Association's existence. He was guest of honour at a dinner held at the Craven Inn, Strand, in October. Fifty boys were present, a cheque was presented to Mr. Marsh for £41 (not such a measly amount at the time) and there were speeches and the singing of "For He's a Jolly Good Fellow". The membership fee was five shillings a year, reduced to half a crown for those under 21. For those over 32 (why 32?) life membership was available for thirty shillings.

Apart from the involvement of Mr. Marsh, there is another odd link between the OHA of 1939 and 1953. The speaker at the prewar Dinner and Dance held in "Ye Mecca", Finsbury Circus, was Old Boy Len Lewsy who gave an interesting and lively speech – "his reference to Cleopatra and Mark Anthony

*An Annual Dinner of the Old Highburians' Association, held in the 1960s with Mr. R.J. King presiding.*

is something which other after dinner speakers might inwardly digest." It would be fascinating to know what that was about. But he turns up again in 1953, paying tribute to Mr. Marsh on behalf of the older Old Boys, except that this time he is described as Major Len Lewzey. He must have been the same Major L.G. Lewzey, MC, TD, who was President of the Defence Surveyors' Association in 1952-54.

The Old Highburians' Association went on under the presidency of Mr. King and then of Dr. Boyson. In 1968 and 1969 it held its Annual Dinner at the Tavistock Banqueting Rooms in Charing Cross Road. The toast to the Association was proposed by teachers Mr. Ward and Mr. Lane respectively. In 1972 the dinner was held at the Alexandra National Hotel in Seven Sisters Road – which many of our readers will probably remember – where the toast to the Association was proposed by Mr. Wood. After this any record of the dinners is lacking. But the Association, or at least the football section, survived into the early 1990s. According to an internet source of videos, the Old Highburians were playing – and losing – matches against the Old Minchendians in March 1991 and the Old Camdenians in February 1992. After this records of the old OHA dry up. It is reported that the Old Highburians Football Club folded in 2000.

## Old Highburians 2001

The new Association came into being in a roundabout way. Some Old Boys had naturally kept in touch and the arrival of internet sites, like "Friends Reunited" helped. Brian Boyle takes up the story:

"Peter Lowe and I have remained friends since we left school although he lives in High Wycombe and I in St. Neots, Cambridgeshire. When Peter suggested over a pint that we should try tracing our former school friends, I was thinking in terms of finding a few who would be still in the area and with whom we might have a quiet drink. We tried initially to get the *Daily Mail* to publish an appeal but without success.

"We then decided to use the internet and clearly we needed to start with the less common names, as there would be too many Smiths and Jones's. Our search led us to John Bonnewell's son, only to find that John had sadly died a few years ago, We also learned of the recent death of Ronald Beverton, the former German teacher, and of Mrs. P. Cobby, the former School Secretary and wife of the French teacher. However, thanks to Gill Whitley's internet service *Searching for a Memory*, we were able to match names from the cast of the 1953 school play, *Morning Departure*. These contacts then led us to others through the school magazines of 1954 and 1955. We also placed an appeal in the Arsenal v Sparta-Prague Champions League programme, which brought forward a few more names. It was a surprise to us that so many still lived in the North London/Hertfordshire area. We really thought more ex-pupils would now live farther afield and, thus, would be very difficult if not impossible to trace. However, Gill's internet service has proved an outstanding success in locating people. What a pity it wasn't around 20 years ago."

By the beginning of 2001, Brian and his fellow organisers had contacted 100 Old Boys and former teachers and it was decided to go ahead with a full reunion, rather than the smaller pub-based gatherings which were already taking place. Seventy-five of the 100 Old Boys, plus 15 guests, attended the group's first Reunion Buffet Lunch, held in the Victory Services Club at Marble Arch on 29 April 2001. It was a great occasion for gossip and catching up, since many had not seen their former classmates for 50 years. One regret was the non-attendance through illness of Lindsey Lanc, the much respected former woodwork master. He died in June 2001, but only weeks before his death had been delighted to see Pat Hartigan, Tom Reid and Peter Read. Tom Reid attended the funeral and a floral tribute was sent on behalf of all ex-pupils.

As the organisers of the 2001 reunion were now holding a not inconsiderable sum of money it was decided to form a committee, appoint officials who could sign cheques, etc., and produce a constitution. For the time being, the committee was self-elected and consisted of Brian Boyle as chairman, Tony Sandell as Hon. Secretary and Pat Hartigan as Hon. Treasurer.

The first AGM was held immediately before the 2002 Reunion Buffet, again located in the Victory Services Club. At this a full committee was elected, consisting of:

| | |
|---|---|
| Hon. President: | Mr. George Cobby |
| Chairman: | Brian Boyle |
| Hon. Secretary: | Anthony Sandell |
| Hon. Treasurer: | Patrick Hartigan |
| Subscriptions: | Alan Watson |
| Newsletter: | Gerry Robinson |

The subsequent AGM in April 2003 decided to set a subscription of £15 p.a. to cover stationery, postage and administration costs, quite apart from the cost of the Reunion and Buffet. The 2003 Reunion also heard a tribute by Mr. Dennis Lewis, former maths master and football coach, to Tony Edelstein who died in early April of that year – a former Head Boy, talented cricketer, family man and fellow-worshipper with Mr. Lewis at the North London Synagogue.

A Roll of Old Highburians records those who have been traced so far. Addresses of most of them appear on the website, _www.old-highburians.org_ . Additions and changes are notified to Brian Boyle, Chairman Old Highburians Association, 2 Reynolds Drive, Little Paxton, St. Neots PE19 6QB.

*Mike Edghill and Brian Boyle at one of their pre-Reunion meetings.*

# A Few Biographies

**Brian Boyle** (1949-56)

Brian worked in Lyons Teashops between leaving school and National Service in the Royal Army Pay Corps. He had a vague idea of becoming a journalist but didn't know how to set about it, so started as a Production Assistant in publishing. He became an estimator with a West London printing house. Brian and his wife, Jill, got married at the height of the London housing boom of 1971-72 which led him to transfer to his firm's Bedford works, and settle in St. Neots. The company went bust in 1975 and Brian changed careers, becoming a buyer in local government. He was given a compulsory early retirement package in 1992 but still does temporary work "to keep the wolf from the door".

**Len Clark CBE** (1927-33)

Len, now 89, is the oldest Old Boy that we have traced. When he joined the school, the Head was Mr. William Spragg, an elderly and over kind figure with more tolerance than discipline. Spragg was replaced by the disciplinarian 'Boggy' Marsh. Len spent his career in the London County Council and its successor, the GLC, finishing as Administrator of the London Ambulance Service. He describes it as "a moderately successful but not very noteworthy career". Outside his full-time job, he became involved with countryside issues. At various times, he was national chairman of the Youth Hostels Association, had a role in most of the committees of the National Trust and was on the Landscape Committee of the Department of Transport. A former Director of the Samaritans, he still works for his local branch.

**Ken Friar OBE**

Ken began working for Arsenal F.C. part-time when he was still a 12 year-old at Highbury County. He went on to become a director and the club's Managing Director, playing a leading role in the planning of Arsenal's new stadium at Ashburton Grove. In October 2004, Ken and manager Arsène Wenger received the Freedom of the London Borough of Islington.

**Patrick Hartigan** (1947-54)

After National Service in the Intelligence Corps, Patrick's first job was repairing electric cloth-cutting machines. Not a lot of people know that. It was only a temporary job and he soon gave it up to work for the Inland Revenue. As if that was not bad enough, he then transferred to the Official Receiver's Department, dealing with company liquidations and bankruptcies. He then moved into the accountancy profession as an insolvency practitioner, becoming President of the Insolvency Practitioners Association in 1993. Yet he never let his work get in the way of his real interest – amateur dramatics. Having learned his craft in the school plays, he joined the St.Paul's Players of Winchmore Hill, with whom he has been regularly treading the boards ever since. Doesn't seem to qualify for the juvenile lead any more, though!

### John Hough (1954-61)

John has spent his career in films, becoming an established and respected film director. Among the many TV series he has directed are *The Avengers, The Prisoner, The Saint* and *Dempsey and Makepiece.* He has directed 17 feature films, including the Disney film, *Escape to Witch Mountain, Biggles* and *Hell House.* John is still directing and is chairman of the British Film Corporation plc, based at Pinewood Studios.

### Victor Pemberton (late 1940s)

Victor was at Highbury in the late 1940s. He has written a series of popular novels, the first of which *Our Family* is a fictionalised story of his own family who lived near the Nag's Head in Holloway. This novel started life as three one-and-a-half hour radio plays. Then came seven novels culminating in *Leo's Girl* which has just been published. A ninth title is due out in the Autumn. Victor is also a successful television writer and producer and has only recently handed over his own production company.  He divides his time between his home in Halstead, Essex and another in Sri Lanka.

### David Perman (1947-54)

After supply teaching in a secondary modern, David became a journalist. He progressed from the *Oxford Mail* via *The Observer* to the BBC World Service where he was variously a writer, producer, editor, Arabic Programme Organiser and head of the Greek Section. He also interviewed King Hussein, Mrs.Thatcher (twice) and the Ayatollah Khomeini. He took early retirement in 1991 when the BBC bureaucracy became too much for him and founded the Rockingham Press which publishes poetry and history books. David's other life is as a conservationist in Ware, Hertfordshire. Here he has managed the restoration of riverside gazebos and the Grade One 18th-century Scott's Grotto, as well as founding the Ware Museum and commissioning public sculptures for the town.

### Tony Sandell (1950-55)

After National Service, where he served in Malaya as a Second Lieutenant attached to the 17th Gurkha Division, Tony joined the Marketing Department of a cosmetics company before moving to a London advertising agency for "a year or two's experience". In 1980 he became Managing Director of Davis, Gibson Advertising which in 1988 he and his partners sold to a worldwide marketing services group. Since then Tony has been involved in seven acquisitions and mergers, the latest resulting in him heading up an account group at TBWA, one of London's biggest and most creative agencies. Tony retired in 2000 after 35 years in the ad agency business. Tony has had a great interest in sport all his life and played football at Finchley FC from 1956-1971. He had the privilege of playing at Highbury Stadium in the Semi-Final of the FA Amateur Cup (Mike Edghill, another Highbury County old boy was in the same team), against Spurs at White Hart Lane and against Chelsea at Stamford Bridge when the referee was none other than Dennis Lewis. Tony captained the Combined Services in Malaya and the London FA. He also represented the Middlesex FA and the Athenian League. He spends his retirement playing golf and, together with his daughters, supporting Arsenal.

## In Memoriam

In the course of searching for old school friends we became aware that a number had sadly passed away. Here we pay our respects to those who are no longer with us:

| | |
|---|---|
| BYE, Donald | died c.1992 |
| BABBS, Ron | died 1995 |
| BONNEWELL, John | died 1995 |
| BEVERTON, Ronald | died 2000 |
| BLUMENTHAL, Philip | died c.1957 |
| COBBY, Mrs. Patricia | died 1997 |
| COLLEY, Michael | died 1991 |
| EDELSTEIN, Tony | died 2003 |
| ENGLEFIELD, Derek | died at a young age |
| FULLWORTH, John | died age unknown |
| HERBERT, Keith | died 1999 |
| LANE, Lindsey | died 2001 |
| PARNALL, Alan | died 2001 |
| SAVIN, Peter | died 2000 |
| SIMPKINS, Albert | died 1996 |
| THOMAS, Anthony | died 1987 |
| THOMAS, Robert | died 1965 |
| WEBSTER, George | died c.1965 |
| WRIGHT, Alfred | died 2004 |
| WOODFORD, Terry | died January 2005 |

# Acknowledgements

*The author and publisher gratefully acknowledge the assistance and provision of material by the following:*

Martin Banham and the staff of Islington Local History Centre, 245 St. John Street, London EC1V 4NB

London Metropolitan Archives, 40 Northampton Road, London EC1R 0HB

The Institute of Historical Research, University of London, publisher of the *Victoria County History of Middlesex*

*Islington Past* by John Richardson (Historical Publications Ltd. – Philimore)

*Images of England: Islington Second Selection* by Gavin Smith (Tempus Publishing Ltd.)

The Hampstead & Highgate Newspaper Group Ltd., publishers of *The Islington Gazette* and *North London Press*

Keith Sugden for information from his book, *History of Highbury*, published by the Islington Archaeology & History Society, 1984